TIMED READINGS

Third Edition

Fifty 400-Word Passages
with Questions for
Building Reading Speed

BOOK NINE

Edward Spargo

JAMESTOWN PUBLISHERS

a division of NTC/CONTEMPORARY PUBLISHING GROUP
Lincolnwood, Illinois USA

Titles in This Series
Timed Readings, Third Edition
Timed Readings in Literature

Teaching Notes are available for this text and
will be sent to the instructor. Please write on
school stationery; tell us what grade
you teach and identify the text.

Timed Readings, Third Edition
Book Nine

Cover and text design: Deborah Hulsey Christie

ISBN: 0-89061-511-X

Published by Jamestown Publishers,
a division of NTC/Contemporary Publishing Group, Inc.,
4255 West Touhy Avenue,
Lincolnwood (Chicago), Illinois 60646-1975 U.S.A.
© 1989 by NTC/Contemporary Publishing Group, Inc.

9 0 GW 11 10 9 8 7

Contents

Introduction to the Student

These *Timed Readings* are designed to help you become a faster and better reader. As you progress through the book, you will find yourself growing in reading speed and comprehension. You will be challenged to increase your reading rate while maintaining a high level of comprehension.

Reading, like most things, improves with practice. If you practice improving your reading speed, you will improve. As you will see, the rewards of improved reading speed will be well worth your time and effort.

Why Read Faster?

The quick and simple answer is that faster readers are better readers. Does this statement surprise you? You might think that fast readers would miss something and their comprehension might suffer. This is not true, for two reasons:

1. Faster readers comprehend faster. When you read faster, the writer's message is coming to you faster and makes sense sooner. Ideas are interconnected. The writer's thoughts are all tied together, each one leading to the next. The more quickly you can see how ideas are related to each other, the more quickly you can comprehend the meaning of what you are reading.

2. Faster readers concentrate better. Concentration is essential for comprehension. If your mind is wandering you can't understand what you are reading. A lack of concentration causes you to re-read, sometimes over and over, in order to comprehend. Faster readers concentrate better because there's less time for distractions to interfere. Comprehension, in turn, contributes to concentration. If you are concentrating and comprehending, you will not become distracted.

Want to Read More?

Do you wish that you could read more? (or, at least, would you like to do your required reading in less time?) Faster reading will help.

The illustration on the next page shows the number of books someone might read over a period of ten years. Let's see what faster reading could do for you. Look at the stack of books read by a slow reader and the stack

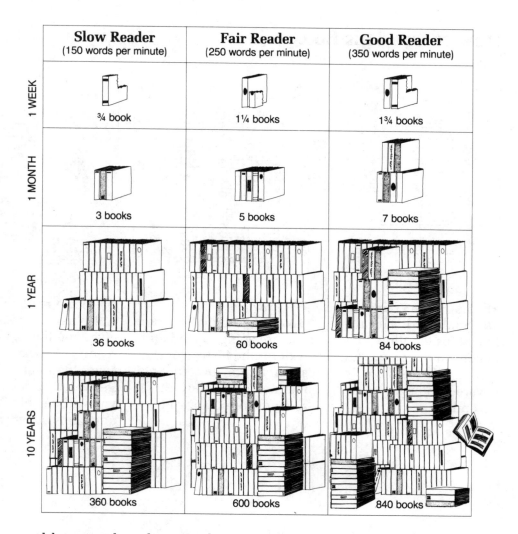

	Slow Reader (150 words per minute)	**Fair Reader** (250 words per minute)	**Good Reader** (350 words per minute)
1 WEEK	¾ book	1¼ books	1¾ books
1 MONTH	3 books	5 books	7 books
1 YEAR	36 books	60 books	84 books
10 YEARS	360 books	600 books	840 books

read by a good reader. (We show a speed of 350 words a minute for our "good" reader, but many fast readers can more than double that speed.) Let's say, however, that you are now reading at a rate of 150 words a minute. The illustration shows you reading 36 books a year. By increasing your reading speed to 250 words a minute, you could increase the number of books to 60 a year.

We have arrived at these numbers by assuming that the readers in our illustration read for one hour a day, six days a week, and that an average book is about 72,000 words long. Many people do not read that much, but they might if they could learn to read better and faster.

Faster reading doesn't *take* time, it *saves* time!

How to Use This Book

1 **Learn the Four Steps** Study and learn the four steps to follow to become a better and faster reader. The steps are covered on pages 9, 10, 11, and 12.

2 **Preview** Turn to the selection you are going to read and wait for the instructor's signal to preview. Your instructor will allow 30 seconds for previewing.

3 **Begin reading** When your instructor gives you the signal, begin reading. Read at a slightly faster-than-normal speed. Read well enough so that you will be able to answer questions about what you have read.

7 **Fill in the progress graph** Enter your score and plot your reading time on the graph on page 118 or 119. The right-hand side of the graph shows your words-per-minute reading speed. Write this number at the bottom of the page on the line labeled *Words per Minute.*

4 **Record your time** When you finish reading, look at the blackboard and note your reading time. Your reading time will be the lowest time remaining on the board, or the next number to be erased. Write this time at the bottom of the page on the line labeled *Reading Time.*

5 **Answer the questions** Answer the ten questions on the next page. There are five fact questions and five thought questions. Pick the *best* answer to each question and put an x in the box beside it.

6 **Correct your answers** Using the Answer Key on pages 116 and 117, correct your work. Circle your wrong answers and put an x in the box you should have marked. Score 10 points for each correct answer. Write your score at the bottom of the page on the line labeled *Comprehension Score.*

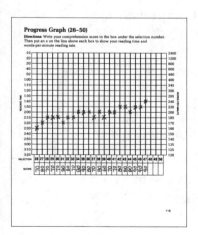

Instructions for the Pacing Drills

From time to time your instructor may wish to conduct pacing drills using *Timed Readings*. For this work you need to use the Pacing Dots printed in the margins of your book pages. The dots will help you regulate your reading speed to match the pace set by your instructor or announced on the reading cassette tape.

> ◣ Pacing Dots

You will be reading at the correct pace if you are at the dot when your instructor says "Mark" or when you hear a tone on the tape. If you are ahead of the pace, read a little more slowly; if you are behind the pace, increase your reading speed. Try to match the pace exactly.

Follow these steps.

Step 1: Record the pace. At the bottom of the page, write on the line labeled *Words per Minute* the rate announced by the instructor or by the speaker on the tape.

Step 2: Begin reading. Wait for the signal to begin reading. Read at a slightly faster-than-normal speed. You will not know how on-target your pace is until you hear your instructor say "Mark" or until you hear the first tone on the tape. After a little practice you will be able to select an appropriate starting speed most of the time.

Step 3: Adjust your pace. As you read, try to match the pace set by the instructor or the tape. Read more slowly or more quickly as necessary. You should be reading the line beside the dot when you hear the pacing signal. The pacing sounds may distract you at first. Don't worry about it. Keep reading and your concentration will return.

Step 4: Stop and answer questions. Stop reading when you are told to, even if you have not finished the selection. Answer the questions right away. Correct your work and record your score on the line *Comprehension Score*. Strive to maintain 80 percent comprehension on each drill as you gradually increase your pace.

Step 5: Fill in the pacing graph. Transfer your words-per-minute rate to the box labeled *Pace* on the pacing graph on page 120. Then plot your comprehension score on the line above the box.

These pacing drills are designed to help you become a more flexible reader. They encourage you to "break out" of a pattern of reading everything at the same speed.

The drills help in other ways, too. Sometimes in a reading program you reach a certain level and bog down. You don't seem able to move on and progress. The pacing drills will help you to work your way out of such slumps and get your reading program moving again.

Steps to Faster Reading

STEP 1: PREVIEW

When you read, do you start in with the first word, or do you look over the whole selection for a moment? Good readers preview the selection first—this helps to make them good, and fast, readers.

1. Read the Title. The first thing to do when previewing is to read the title of the selection. Titles are designed not only to announce the subject, but also to make the reader think. What can you learn from the title? What thoughts does it bring to mind? What do you already know about this subject?

2. Read the Opening Paragraph. If the first paragraph is long, read the first sentence or two instead. The first paragraph is the writer's opportunity to greet the reader. He may have something to tell you about what is to come. Some writers announce what they hope to tell you in the selection. Some writers tell why they are writing. Some writers just try to get the reader's attention—they may ask a provocative question.

3. Read the Closing Paragraph. If the last paragraph is long, read just the final line or two. The closing paragraph is the writer's last chance to talk to his reader. He may have something important to say at the end. Some writers repeat the main idea once more. Some writers draw a conclusion: this is what they have been leading up to. Some writers summarize their thoughts; they tie all the facts together.

4. Glance Through. Scan the selection quickly to see what else you can pick up. Discover whatever you can to help you read the selection. Are there names, dates, numbers? If so, you may have to read more slowly. Are there colorful adjectives? The selection might be light and fairly easy to read. Is the selection informative, containing a lot of facts, or conversational, an informal discussion with the reader?

flying normal towers stage migration. some cruising pelicans, time subtle scientists close

Steps to Faster Reading

STEP 2: READ FOR MEANING

When you read, do you just see words? Are you so occupied reading words that you sometimes fail to get the meaning? Good readers see beyond the words—they read for meaning. This makes them faster readers.

1. Build Concentration. You cannot read with understanding if you are not concentrating. Every reader's mind wanders occasionally; it is not a cause for alarm. When you discover that your thoughts have strayed, correct the situation right away. The longer you wait, the harder it becomes. Avoid distractions and distracting situations. Outside noises and activities will compete for your attention if you let them. Keep the preview information in mind as you read. This will help to focus your attention on the selection.

2. Read in Thought Groups. Individual words do not tell us much. They must be combined with other words in order to yield meaning. To obtain meaning from the printed page, therefore, the reader should see the words in meaningful combinations. If you see only a word at a time (called word-by-word reading), your comprehension suffers along with your speed. To improve both speed and comprehension, try to group the words into phrases which have a natural relationship to each other. For practice, you might want to read aloud, trying to speak the words in meaningful combinations.

3. Question the Author. To sustain the pace you have set for yourself, and to maintain a high level of comprehension, question the writer as you read. Continually ask yourself such questions as, "What does this mean? What is he saying now? How can I use this information?" Questions like these help you to concentrate fully on the selection.

Steps to Faster Reading

STEP 3: GRASP PARAGRAPH SENSE

The paragraph is the basic unit of meaning. If you can discover quickly and understand the main point of each paragraph, you can comprehend the author's message. Good readers know how to find the main ideas of paragraphs quickly. This helps to make them faster readers.

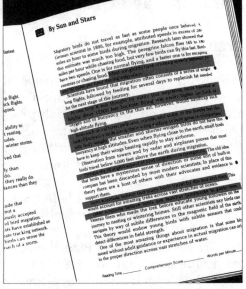

1. Find the Topic Sentence. The topic sentence, the sentence containing the main idea, is often the first sentence of a paragraph. It is followed by other sentences which support, develop, or explain the main idea. Sometimes a topic sentence comes at the end of a paragraph. When it does, the supporting details come first, building the base for the topic sentence. Some paragraphs do not have a topic sentence. Such paragraphs usually create a mood or feeling, rather than present information.

2. Understand Paragraph Structure. Every well-written paragraph has purpose. The purpose may be to inform, define, explain, persuade, compare or contrast, illustrate, and so on. The purpose should always relate to the main idea and expand on it. As you read each paragraph, see how the body of the paragraph is used to tell you more about the main idea or topic sentence. Read the supporting details intelligently, recognizing that what you are reading is all designed to develop the single main idea.

Steps to Faster Reading

STEP 4: ORGANIZE FACTS

When you read, do you tend to see a lot of facts without any apparent connection or relationship? Understanding how the facts all fit together to deliver the author's message is, after all, the reason for reading. Good readers organize facts as they read. This helps them to read rapidly and well.

1. Discover the Writer's Plan. Look for a clue or signal word early in the article which might reveal the author's structure. Every writer has a plan or outline which he follows. If the reader can discover his method of organization, he has the key to understanding the message. Sometimes the author gives you obvious signals. If he says, "There are three reasons . . ." the wise reader looks for a listing of the three items. Other less obvious signal words such as *moreover, otherwise, consequently* all tell the reader the direction the writer's message will take.

2. Relate as You Read. As you read the selection, keep the information learned during the preview in mind. See how the ideas you are reading all fit into place. Consciously strive to relate what you are reading to the title. See how the author is carrying through in his attempt to piece together a meaningful message. As you discover the relationship among the ideas, the message comes through quickly and clearly.

Timed
Reading
Selections

Virtually every American can recognize a dollar bill at a mere glance. Many can identify it by its sound or texture. But few people indeed can accurately describe the world's most powerful, important currency.

The American dollar bill measures 2⅝″ by 6⅛″, with a thickness of .0043″. It is colored with black ink on one side and green on the other; the exact composition of the paper and ink is a closely guarded government secret. Despite its weighty importance, the dollar bill actually weighs little. It requires nearly 500 bills to tip the scales at a pound. Not only is the ● dollar bill lightweight, but it also has a brief life span. Few dollar bills survive longer than 18 months.

The word "dollar" is taken from the German word "taler," the name for the world's most important currency in the 16th century. The taler was a silver coin first minted in 1518 under the reign of Charles V, Emperor of Germany.

The concept of paper money is a relatively recent innovation in the history of American currency. When the Constitution was signed, people had little regard for paper money because of its steadily decreasing value during the colonial era. Because of this lack of faith, the new American ● government minted only coins for common currency. Interest-bearing bank notes were issued at the same time, but their purpose was limited to providing money for urgent government crises, such as American involvement in the War of 1812.

The first noninterest-bearing paper currency was authorized by Congress in 1862, at the height of the Civil War. At this point, citizens' old fears of devalued paper currency had calmed, and the dollar bill was born. The new green colored paper money quickly earned the nickname "greenback."

Today, the American dollar bill is a product of the Federal Reserve, and ● is issued from the twelve Federal Reserve banks around the United States. The government keeps a steady supply of approximately two billion bills in circulation at all times.

Controversy continues to surround the true value of the dollar bill. American history has seen generations of politicians argue in favor of a gold standard for American currency. However, for the present, the American dollar bill holds the value that is printed on it, and little more. The only other guarantee on the bill is a Federal Reserve pledge of collateral in the form of government securities.

Recalling Facts

1. Most dollar bills remain in circulation for
   - ☐ a. 6 months.
   - ☐ b. 18 months.
   - ☐ c. 3 years.

2. The first American paper money was issued in
   - ☐ a. 1812.
   - ☐ b. 1826.
   - ☐ c. 1862.

3. Today's dollar bills are issued from the
   - ☐ a. U.S. Congress.
   - ☐ b. Franklin Mint.
   - ☐ c. Federal Reserve.

4. The "taler" was
   - ☐ a. the first American interest-bearing bank note.
   - ☐ b. a German silver coin used in the 1500s.
   - ☐ c. a nickname for the first dollar bill.

5. How many banks belong to the Federal Reserve?
   - ☐ a. 10
   - ☐ b. 12
   - ☐ c. 16

Understanding the Passage

6. In the post colonial era, the government used only coins for currency because
   - ☐ a. citizens had little faith in paper money.
   - ☐ b. coins were cheaper to produce.
   - ☐ c. it was more difficult to counterfeit coins.

7. Interest-bearing bank notes were issued in the early 1800s for the purpose of
   - ☐ a. giving citizens a sound investment.
   - ☐ b. collecting funds for government crises.
   - ☐ c. trying out a paper currency.

8. The author implies paper money
   - ☐ a. has questionable value.
   - ☐ b. is preferable to a gold standard.
   - ☐ c. continues to inspire controversy.

9. The author states that the concept of paper money is
   - ☐ a. a relatively recent innovation.
   - ☐ b. an idea with a 400-year history.
   - ☐ c. based on the German taler.

10. We can infer that coins are no longer the principal currency because
    - ☐ a. paper money has more intrinsic value.
    - ☐ b. they are too expensive to produce.
    - ☐ c. they are too easily copied.

2 Angioplasty

People with heart disease now have shorter hospital stays thanks to innovations in medical technology. One important change is a modern non-surgical procedure called angioplasty. The method is used to treat some patients with coronary artery disease, or CAD.

A symptom of CAD is a narrowing of the arteries. This is usually caused by the build-up of a waxy material called plaque. Each artery supplies the heart with oxygen-rich blood and feeds a specific part of the heart. When the arteries are narrowed, too little oxygen-rich blood reaches the heart, causing chest pain.

Angioplasty improves the relay of blood to the heart by expanding the constricted passageway. A balloon device is inserted at the narrowed point of the diseased artery. The balloon is inflated and the artery returns to its proper width, improving the flow of oxygen-rich blood.

Before a patient undergoes angioplasty, he must first go through routine tests and X-rays to assure his condition is prime for the procedure. Then the patient receives medications to help him relax, as well as a local anesthesia to deaden the nerve endings at the point where the balloon device is introduced to the body. The patient remains conscious throughout the procedure.

When the procedure begins, the guiding device is inserted in an artery in either the groin or arm. A dye that is sensitive to X-ray is injected into the artery so that the physician can view the narrowed artery more clearly. The physician then guides the balloon device through the narrowed artery with the help of a guidewire and an X-ray monitor. When the balloon reaches the narrowed point of the artery it is inflated for 20 to 60 seconds. It is then deflated and inflated several more times until the waxy build-up is compressed against the lining of the artery and the passageway is expanded.

Once the artery's path is cleared, the physician checks to make certain the flow of blood has improved. The guiding device is then removed. The entire procedure takes about two hours.

The patient is required to remain still for a period of several hours following the procedure in order to discourage bleeding. But within 12 to 24 hours many patients are able to walk unassisted and without chest pain.

Though angioplasty does not cure CAD, it offers a relatively quick and simple method of relief to patients who suffer from heart disease.

Recalling Facts

1. CAD stands for
   - ☐ a. cardial arterial disease.
   - ☐ b. coronary artery disease.
   - ☐ c. coronary angioplasty disease.

2. Angioplasty is a
   - ☐ a. procedure.
   - ☐ b. device.
   - ☐ c. cure.

3. Dye is used to help
   - ☐ a. widen the narrowed artery.
   - ☐ b. the physician view the narrowed artery.
   - ☐ c. sensitize the patient's heart.

4. Throughout the procedure, the patient is
   - ☐ a. unconscious.
   - ☐ b. partially conscious.
   - ☐ c. conscious.

5. During angioplasty, the balloon remains inflated for
   - ☐ a. 20 to 60 seconds.
   - ☐ b. 20 to 60 minutes.
   - ☐ c. two hours.

Understanding the Passage

6. CAD is characterized by
   - ☐ a. an excess of oxygen-rich blood in the heart.
   - ☐ b. a diminished number of red blood cells.
   - ☐ c. a narrowing of the arteries.

7. The purpose of angioplasty is to
   - ☐ a. improve the flow of blood to the heart.
   - ☐ b. cure heart disease.
   - ☐ c. give a clear view of the patient's heart.

8. Chest pain sometimes occurs when the
   - ☐ a. arteries don't inflate.
   - ☐ b. heart receives too little blood.
   - ☐ c. arteries don't build up enough plaque.

9. The author implies angioplasty is
   - ☐ a. an expensive procedure..
   - ☐ b. an innovative procedure.
   - ☐ c. dangerous to perform.

10. The author implies that angioplasty affects the
    - ☐ a. length of stay in hospitals.
    - ☐ b. patient's likelihood of future heart disease.
    - ☐ c. development of plaque in the arteries.

3 Comets

Among the most spectacular visions in the sky is the glowing trail of a ball of frozen gases commonly known as the comet. Comets are comprised of water, ammonia, methane, and carbon dioxide and are held together by small fragments of rock and metallic materials. They are created in outer space, beyond the reaches of our solar system. They are seen fairly infrequently but are nonetheless plentiful—over two million comets reportedly travel through our solar system.

Comets appear small but are in fact enormous. Some are larger than the sun, but most are approximately the size of Jupiter. Many comets follow elongated orbits and are visible only when they are within Saturn's orbit. As comets travel through the solar system toward the sun, solar energy vaporizes their gases, producing a blazing head, called the coma. Some comets also develop a tail, which can extend millions of miles. Despite their large scale, comets are believed to weigh relatively little, probably less than one billionth the earth's mass.

Early astronomers found that as comets orbited the sun, a tail was created as solar energy forced the coma's particles out. Today's scientists have confirmed these beliefs, and have further identified two solar forces at work in the creation of a comet's tail. Radiation pressure is responsible for pushing the dust particles away from the coma, and solar wind moves the coma's ionized gases.

As the comet travels away from the sun, the tail begins to disappear due to condensation of the gases. Once these gases are separated from the comet, they are lost forever. As a result, most comets survive only 100 close orbits of the sun. When all the comet's gases have been released, all that is left of the comet is a bundle of stone and metal particles, which continues to orbit without a coma or tail.

Perhaps the most famous comet is Halley's comet, which appears once every 76 years. The Chinese have recorded all of Halley's appearances since 240 B.C. The comet's 1910 sighting was remarkable for its clear visibility; it could be seen in daylight, and was observed to have developed a tail nearly one million miles long. The 1986 appearance of Halley's comet was disappointing because it was extremely difficult to see from the Northern hemisphere. However, Halley's next sighting is expected to be spectacular—in the year 2062.

Recalling Facts

1. Comets are formed
   - ☐ a. on other planets.
   - ☐ b. in outer space.
   - ☐ c. from solar energy.

2. Most comets are the size of
   - ☐ a. the sun.
   - ☐ b. Saturn.
   - ☐ c. Jupiter.

3. Most comets are visible only when they are within the orbit of
   - ☐ a. Saturn.
   - ☐ b. earth.
   - ☐ c. the sun.

4. Most comets survive close orbits of the sun
   - ☐ a. only once.
   - ☐ b. 10 times.
   - ☐ c. 100 times.

5. Halley's comet was first recorded by the Chinese in
   - ☐ a. 1910.
   - ☐ b. 76 B.C.
   - ☐ c. 240 B.C.

Understanding the Passage

6. Comets are held together by
   - ☐ a. water and ammonia.
   - ☐ b. rock and metallic fragments.
   - ☐ c. methane and carbon dioxide.

7. The comet's coma is developed when
   - ☐ a. solar energy vaporizes the comet's gases.
   - ☐ b. the comet's orbit travels away from the sun.
   - ☐ c. the comet enters the solar system.

8. Radiation pressure is the solar force which
   - ☐ a. creates the coma's ionized gases.
   - ☐ b. pushes dust particles away from the coma.
   - ☐ c. causes the comet to orbit.

9. A comet's tail disappears when
   - ☐ a. its gases condense.
   - ☐ b. its dust particles expand.
   - ☐ c. the comet travels toward the sun.

10. The 1910 sighting of Halley's comet was remarkable in part because of its
    - ☐ a. enlarged coma.
    - ☐ b. brief appearance.
    - ☐ c. visibility in daylight.

Conservation: The Future Is Now

Modern technology has developed in a manner which often conflicts with the environment. Nevertheless, it is possible and practical to achieve a high level of technology without altering the overall environment or depleting non-renewable natural resources.

There are two basic methods of conserving the natural environment. One is *alternative technology* in which techniques (such as windmills and solar energy) must be found for providing power in a more decentralized manner. The other is to try to minimize the effects of modern technology by the more efficient use of materials and more effective pollution control. The differences between the two approaches depend upon whether today's megalopolis is too large to be economical. There comes a point when the quality of life can no longer be improved because of the high population density and the largely unsuccessful attempts to meet its demands.

Present energy policies of the western world are considering new energy sources to meet the demands of a growing population. The main sources used have been oil, gas, and coal—which are in limited supply—and nuclear power, which has problems concerning radioactive waste storage. Geothermal, hydroelectric, hydrothermal, wind, and solar energy are all alternative possibilities, but only solar energy is likely to become a main power source for many countries.

Many of the materials used daily in a technological society are destined to be discarded. Rags, paper, metal, glass, and plastics are all substances that could be recycled or reused. For example, ground glass can be used for road surfacing. Many industrial residues, like slag and ash, can be used in the same way, or as building materials. Research is being done to determine methods of separating useful products from industrial and domestic waste. Plastics and organic materials contain hydrocarbons which could be used for making gas and oil and are presently destroyed by burning. Extracting these commodities from waste may be vital in the future, considering that oil and gas are non-renewable natural resources.

The processing of sewerage requires considerable amounts of electricity. Vast quantities of sewerage have to be pumped and treated daily and several megawatts of power are needed for the task. Many sewerage treatment plants in the U.S. have become self-sufficient by using the methane gas given off by sewerage. This is collected in gas holders and burned to produce heat and create electricity. The solid waste itself is often used for soil enrichment.

Recalling Facts

1. Which of the following substances cannot be reused or recycled?
   □ a. paper
   □ b. nuclear waste
   □ c. oil

2. Which form of alternative energy will probably be most used in the future?
   □ a. hydroelectric
   □ b. geothermal
   □ c. solar energy

3. Processing sewerage requires large quantities of
   □ a. water.
   □ b. electricity.
   □ c. gas.

4. Plastics and organic materials contain
   □ a. hydrocarbons.
   □ b. methane gas.
   □ c. slag.

5. Recycled ground glass can be used for
   □ a. window panes.
   □ b. road surfacing.
   □ c. mirrors.

Understanding the Passage

6. From this selection, we can determine that
   □ a. conservation technology is a necessity.
   □ b. nuclear power is the energy source of the future.
   □ c. problems of energy conservation are not worldwide.

7. Alternative technology suggests that
   □ a. new ways be found to burn coal, oil, and gas.
   □ b. solar energy and wind power be considered.
   □ c. new ways be found to store radioactive waste.

8. Methane gas is used to
   □ a. conserve industrial residues.
   □ b. create recycled paper products.
   □ c. provide electricity to process sewerage.

9. Recycled forms of industrial waste used for building materials are
   □ a. ash and slag.
   □ b. paper and glass.
   □ c. plastic and metal.

10. Modern technology is detrimental to the natural environment because
   □ a. of industrial pollutants.
   □ b. it has become too expensive.
   □ c. it has become too complicated.

5 The Morse Code

Samuel Finley Breese Morse was a talented artist and teacher who became famous for an invention that sprang from a hobby. He invented the telegraph. Morse financed his innovation by painting and teaching art at New York University. Despite the discouraging comments of his fellow professors, Morse toiled at the telegraph until it was perfected. The next problem was to create a vocabulary for his invention—a special language without words.

Morse's idea was to have an alphabet made entirely of symbols which could be sent over a telegraph wire, thereby hastening the transmission of messages. He came up with a system of dots and dashes which could be "tapped" on the telegraph, arranged in combinations to represent every letter in the alphabet.

The United States Congress became curious about this invention and invited Morse to Capitol Hill for a demonstration of his telegraph on May 24, 1844. Morse demonstrated his skills by sending a message from Washington, D.C., to Baltimore. That message, "What hath God wrought?" was successfully transmitted and received, and a new era in communications technology was born.

Today, the Morse Code is so widely used that it is no longer considered a secret language. One advantage to the code, despite its seeming mystery, is that a variety of "telegraph" instruments may be used—finger tapping, buzzers, whistles, lights, and even flags.

Flag transmission is relatively simple to perform, but it requires special equipment. In areas with dark backgrounds, a white flag with a small square of red in the center is preferred. Conversely, in areas featuring a light background, a dark colored flag with a small square of white in the center is most efficient.

The flag code involves three movements, all of which begin and end with the flag being held perpendicular in front of the sender. A dot is created by swinging the flag down to the right and back in position; a dash is made by swinging the flag down to the left and back. An interval is created by waving the flag down in front and back in position. There are no pauses between dots and dashes, but pauses are used to indicate the end of a letter. One interval indicates the end of a word, two signify the end of a sentence, and three intervals indicate the message's end.

Morse Code is thus remarkable not only for its efficiency, but also for its versatility and relative ease of use.

Recalling Facts

1. Aside from inventing Morse Code, Samuel F. B. Morse was also famous for
   - ☐ a. inventing the telegraph.
   - ☐ b. being elected to Congress.
   - ☐ c. teaching art history.

2. The first telegraph message was sent from Washington, D.C., to
   - ☐ a. New York.
   - ☐ b. Baltimore.
   - ☐ c. Philadelphia.

3. Morse first demonstrated his telegraph to Congress in
   - ☐ a. 1824.
   - ☐ b. 1844.
   - ☐ c. 1864.

4. Against a dark background, the best flag to use for Morse Code is
   - ☐ a. solid white.
   - ☐ b. red with a small white square.
   - ☐ c. white with a small red square.

5. A flag wave down to the right indicates
   - ☐ a. an interval.
   - ☐ b. a dot.
   - ☐ c. a dash.

Understanding the Passage

6. Morse financed his invention in part by
   - ☐ a. teaching art.
   - ☐ b. painting houses.
   - ☐ c. working as a messenger.

7. The purpose of Morse Code was to provide
   - ☐ a. the military with a secret language.
   - ☐ b. a language for people who couldn't speak.
   - ☐ c. a means of sending messages by telegraph.

8. Morse was invited to Capitol Hill for the purpose of
   - ☐ a. testifying before Congress.
   - ☐ b. demonstrating the telegraph.
   - ☐ c. revealing his secret code to Congress.

9. We can infer that Morse Code
   - ☐ a. made Morse an important political figure.
   - ☐ b. transformed the world of communications technology.
   - ☐ c. was the forerunner of the telephone.

10. The author states that an advantage of Morse Code is its
    - ☐ a. military application.
    - ☐ b. mysterious meaning.
    - ☐ c. ease of use.

6   Via Satellite

Space research has greatly benefited the field of communications. International television is relayed around the globe by a network of communications satellites orbiting thousands of miles above the earth. International television affords a living room view of such events as the Olympic games—first in 1964 from Tokyo, then in 1968 from Mexico. In 1972 we saw the winter Olympics from Sappora, Japan, and the summer games from Munich, Germany. Today, we simply take it for granted that everything from newscasts in Perth to live performances in Paris will come to our living rooms.

International TV had its debut on July 10, 1962, when many expectant viewers in the United States, and a few in France and England, watched a taped black-and-white picture of an American flag flapping in the Maine breeze to the recorded accompaniment of the "Star Spangled Banner." Picture and sound, transmitted skyward over the Atlantic from a large horn-shaped antenna near Andover, Maine, were being transmitted back to Andover and to Holmdel, N.J., from a new earth satellite, Telstar 1, launched by NASA 15 hours earlier from Cape Canaveral, Florida.

The following day the 170-pound Telstar 1, speeding around the globe every 158 minutes, relayed the first TV pictures westward from Europe, black and whites from both France and England, and within a week the first in color. Two weeks later mass audiences on both sides of the Atlantic watched the first international exchange of live TV. Viewers in Europe saw the Statue of Liberty, a baseball game between the Phillies and the Cubs in Chicago, a Presidential press conference, buffalo roaming the South Dakota plains, and the Mormon Tabernacle Choir singing at Mount Rushmore. Americans, in turn, were able to glimpse Big Ben from London's Tower Bridge, the Coliseum in Rome, the Louvre in Paris, the Sistine Chapel in Vatican City, Sicilian fishermen reefing their nets, and reindeer near the Arctic Circle in Norway.

Other prominent international events seen here by relay from communications satellites were Pope Paul XI's coronation at the Vatican, Winston Churchill's funeral in London, the induction of Prince Charles at Carnarvon, Wales, the opening of Expo 70 in Japan, and President Nixon's visits to China and the Soviet Union. Most common of all are the daily broadcasts of spot news from crucial localities all over the world. Millions of Americans now watch them on their TV screens with little thought about the significant credit line, "via satellite."

Recalling Facts

1. The first international television broadcast was made in
   - ☐ a. 1958.
   - ☐ b. 1962.
   - ☐ c. 1968.

2. The first international television broadcast was
   - ☐ a. filmed.
   - ☐ b. live.
   - ☐ c. taped.

3. The antenna that transmitted the first international broadcast is located in
   - ☐ a. New York.
   - ☐ b. Massachusetts.
   - ☐ c. Maine.

4. The first communications satellite was named
   - ☐ a. Telstar.
   - ☐ b. Spacecom.
   - ☐ c. Tiros.

5. How much time elapsed between the first black and white transmission and color transmission?
   - ☐ a. one week
   - ☐ b. one month
   - ☐ c. one year

Understanding the Passage

6. The first communications satellite
   - ☐ a. was put into operation at once.
   - ☐ b. required many days of testing before it could be used.
   - ☐ c. experienced several technical difficulties at first.

7. The author states that today satellite pictures are
   - ☐ a. viewed with displeasure.
   - ☐ b. difficult to watch.
   - ☐ c. taken for granted.

8. The initial broadcasts between Europe and America showed that
   - ☐ a. countries can cooperate with space launchings.
   - ☐ b. much effort went into achieving variety in sights and sounds.
   - ☐ c. television is more popular in America than in Europe.

9. In this article, the author discusses the
   - ☐ a. functions of the communications satellite.
   - ☐ b. types of programs beamed across the Atlantic.
   - ☐ c. purposes of the Conference on International Television.

10. We can conclude that
    - ☐ a. television programs may originate from any place in the world.
    - ☐ b. only spectacular events are broadcast via satellite.
    - ☐ c. the United States spends more on satellites than any other country.

The Early Navigator's Best Friend

The astrolabe is an ancient astronomical instrument which served many uses concerned with predicting and measuring the positions of the stars and sun. The term literally translates as "star-taker."

The basic and earliest type is the planispheric astrolabe invented by either the Greeks or Alexandrians in the first century B.C. and later perfected by the Arabs. It's a simple model of the earth and sky reduced to two flat brass disks up to ten inches across. One plate depicts the earth and is demarcated with lines of longitude, latitude, the observer's horizon, and other lines indicating angles above the horizon. Since it was be designed for use at a particular latitude, it was customary to furnish several plates.

The other disk is called the rete, from the Latin for net, and it's a simple map of the sky, with the position of bright stars shown by curved pointers. The line of the ecliptic, which determines the sun's path among the stars, (or zodiac), is also marked.

These two disks are mounted on a third disk called the mater, which has a scale of hours around the outside. The rete is free to rotate about the center of this disk. The mater can be set to show the appearance of the sky for any time or date. A sighting device called an alidade is mounted on the same spindle but on the back of the mater, which has a degree scale marked around its outer edge. This facilitates the measuring of the actual position of the sun.

The astolabe was originally used to find the time of day, the rising and setting times of the sun and stars, and even the direction of Mecca before astronomical tables and almanacs were widely used by mariners and other travelers. For people far more dependent on the stars, sun, and astrology, the astrolabe was invaluable. When mechanical clocks became more reliable and astronomical calculations more accurate, the astrolabe became nearly obsolete, although it was still being used in the Arab world until the 19th century. It was extensively used in western Europe in the Middle Ages; Chaucer wrote a well-known "Treatise on the Astrolabe" in 1391. Even after it was outmoded in the later Middle Ages, it was still a fashionable device for travelers and collectors. Although the elegant and elaborate classical instruments are rare, a less complex type of astrolabe can still be purchased today.

Recalling Facts

1. How many flat disks did an astrolabe usually have?
   - ☐ a. three
   - ☐ b. four
   - ☐ c. two

2. The term *rete* comes from the Latin and means
   - ☐ a. disk.
   - ☐ b. net.
   - ☐ c. astrolabe.

3. The astrolabe was probably invented by the
   - ☐ a. Greeks.
   - ☐ b. Arabs.
   - ☐ c. Egyptians.

4. The sighting device of an astrolabe is called
   - ☐ a. a rete.
   - ☐ b. the mater.
   - ☐ c. an alidade.

5. The ecliptic line on the rete represented the
   - ☐ a. sun's path.
   - ☐ b. stars' path.
   - ☐ c. earth's path.

Understanding the Passage

6. The astrolabe was used to determine the
   - ☐ a. time of day.
   - ☐ b. weather.
   - ☐ c. direction of land.

7. A "Treatise on the Astrolabe" was written by a
   - ☐ a. Greek.
   - ☐ b. European.
   - ☐ c. Arab.

8. A nineteenth century Arab might have used an astrolabe to
   - ☐ a. tell time.
   - ☐ b. determine the weather.
   - ☐ c. predict the phase of the moon.

9. Mechanical clocks were responsible for the
   - ☐ a. introduction of the astrolabe.
   - ☐ b. demise of the astrolabe.
   - ☐ c. popularity of the astrolabe.

10. Early extant astrolabes are now considered to be
    - ☐ a. worthless objects of curiosity.
    - ☐ b. valuable items of interest.
    - ☐ c. invaluable to modern mariners.

The Language of Nature

Hikers exploring North America's trails often rely upon celestial bodies and compasses to recover from a lost sense of direction. But in overcast weather, lost travelers can benefit from an old Indian technique for determining direction through the special language of trees.

To follow the guidance of nature's compass, one must locate several trees growing in an exposed area; their foliage, tops, bark, and moss will indicate which direction to pursue. The first step is to determine which side of the tree has the most leaves and branches growing on it. In the northern hemisphere, most trees have the greatest amount of foliage growing on the south side. Tree tops are another important indicator of direction because they almost always incline to the south or southeast. And the northern side of trees ordinarily features bark that is darker and duller in appearance.

If fully grown trees are difficult to locate, tree stumps' ring patterns frequently reveal direction. The north side usually features thicker rings, the southern exposure, thinner rings. Also, regions characterized by heavy precipitation are virtually guaranteed to have trees covered with moss or lichen. These mossy growths, which are velvety to the touch and colored green or brown, customarily grow on the northern side of trees.

The reason trees provide a virtual roadmap for the lost traveler is not mysterious. Sunlight is the key ingredient for the growth of foliage. In the northern hemisphere, most sunlight falls on trees' southern exposure, which in turn creates bigger branches, denser foliage, and more leaves. Also, trees have a natural propensity to reach for sunlight. Hence, the southern side of a tree usually features branches with a horizontal growth pattern, away from the trunk. Branches on the northern side also reach for sunlight, and they tend to point upward, arcing toward the trunk. Also, moisture retention is greater on the northern exposure of a tree because of the relatively diminished amount of sunlight; therefore, more moss growth is likely to appear on a tree's north side.

Climate is yet another important ingredient in the scheme of nature's roadmap. Deciduous trees, which shed leaves seasonally, prosper on slopes which are warmer. In the northern hemisphere, that means that slopes which face south are more likely to have trees that lose leaves.

Clearly, nature is full of signposts and landmarks to help prevent travelers from losing their way. The key is to learn the language of trees.

Recalling Facts

1. Tree bark exposed to the north tends to have
   - ☐ a. thin rings.
   - ☐ b. denser foliage.
   - ☐ c. a dark, dull appearance.

2. Ring patterns in stumps help reveal direction by their
   - ☐ a. circumference.
   - ☐ b. color.
   - ☐ c. thickness.

3. The key ingredient to the growth of foliage is
   - ☐ a. sunlight.
   - ☐ b. moisture.
   - ☐ c. heat.

4. Moss is an indication of
   - ☐ a. arid climatology.
   - ☐ b. southern exposure.
   - ☐ c. moisture retention.

5. Deciduous trees feature
   - ☐ a. excessive branches.
   - ☐ b. seasonal leaf loss.
   - ☐ c. growths of lichen.

Understanding the Passage

6. Trees are particularly useful as directional signposts in
   - ☐ a. cold temperatures.
   - ☐ b. overcast weather.
   - ☐ c. flat terrain.

7. Sunlight produces the greatest amount of foliage on
   - ☐ a. deciduous trees.
   - ☐ b. the south side of trees.
   - ☐ c. moss-covered trees.

8. Deciduous trees prosper on slopes which
   - ☐ a. face south.
   - ☐ b. retain moisture.
   - ☐ c. feature lichen.

9. Tree branches have a natural tendency to
   - ☐ a. grow symmetrically.
   - ☐ b. reach for sunlight.
   - ☐ c. shed leaves in winter.

10. We can infer that
    - ☐ a. a northern direction is indicated by thick clusters of trees.
    - ☐ b. trees are preferable to compasses for providing direction.
    - ☐ c. dense foliage appears most often on the south side of trees.

9 | Finding Gold

Gold can be found in many different kinds of rock and in many geological environments. It is often found with other metals. In fact, more than one third of the gold produced in the United States is a byproduct from mining other metallic ores. Where base metals are deposited, either in veins or as scattered mineral grains, minor amounts of gold are usually deposited with them. Deposits of this type are mined for the predominant metals, but during processing of the ore, the gold is also recovered.

Some deposits of base metals are so large that even though they contain only a small amount of gold per ton, so much is mined that a substantial amount of gold is recovered. Gold recovered from copper ore mined at the vast open-pit mine at Bingham, Utah, for example, almost equals the amount of gold produced from the largest gold mine in the United States.

Geologists study all the factors that control the origin and emplacement of mineral deposits, including gold. Studies of igneous rocks in the field and in the laboratory lead to an understanding of how they came to their present location, how they crystallized to solid rock, and how mineral-bearing solutions and gases formed within them. Studies of rock structures, such as folds, faults, fractures, and joints, and of the effects of heat and pressure on rocks suggest why and where fracturing of the crust took place and where veins might be found. Knowledge of the physical and chemical characteristics of rocks yields information on the pattern of fractures and where to look for them. Studies of weathering processes and transport of material by water enable geologists to predict the most likely places for placer deposits to form.

Research on prospecting methods has led to the development of chemical and spectrographic laboratories that are fitted with newly designed analytical instruments capable of detecting and rapidly measuring the amounts of gold and other valuable metals that may be present in the rocks and ores. These laboratories can accompany the geologist into the field and, by providing on-the-spot analyses of selected samples, guide the geologist in his search.

The occurrence of gold is not capricious; its presence in various kinds of rocks and formation under differing environmental conditions follow natural laws. As geologists increase their knowledge of the ore-forming processes they can expect to improve their ability to find the gold.

*Reading Time*_____ *Comprehension Score*_____ *Words per Minute*_____   31

Recalling Facts

1. What fraction of the United States' gold is a byproduct from mining other ores?
   - ☐ a. one-fourth
   - ☐ b. one-third
   - ☐ c. one-half

2. The United States has a large open-pit copper mine in
   - ☐ a. Alabama.
   - ☐ b. Mississippi.
   - ☐ c. Utah.

3. What type of rock formation reveals the origins of other rocks?
   - ☐ a. igneous
   - ☐ b. extrusive
   - ☐ c. plutonic

4. The occurrence of gold is not
   - ☐ a. common.
   - ☐ b. capricious.
   - ☐ c. geological.

5. Geologists are trying to improve their ability to
   - ☐ a. find gold.
   - ☐ b. refine metals.
   - ☐ c. understand minerals.

Understanding the Passage

6. The author suggests that
   - ☐ a. the occurrence of gold does not follow natural laws.
   - ☐ b. the quality of base metal is improved if it is near gold.
   - ☐ c. heat and pressure have a great effect on creating minerals.

7. Geologists limit their study to the
   - ☐ a. prediction of the location of gold deposits.
   - ☐ b. development of gold recovery techniques.
   - ☐ c. origins and locations of mineral deposits.

8. Spectrographic laboratories
   - ☐ a. record faults and fractures as they occur.
   - ☐ b. study weathering processes that affect mineral formations.
   - ☐ c. measure the amount of precious metals in base ore.

9. Spectrographic laboratories are really
   - ☐ a. mobile units for work in the field.
   - ☐ b. massive structures of complicated technology.
   - ☐ c. branch laboratories of colleges and universities.

10. We can conclude from this selection that
    - ☐ a. most smelting plants are not equipped to recover gold.
    - ☐ b. many people do not recognize gold in base ore.
    - ☐ c. much gold is lost in inefficient mining operations.

10   Mecca and the Muslims

Mecca is the holiest city in the religion of Islam and the birthplace of Mohammed, the religion's founder and prophet. Islam originated in 622 A.D., the year of Mohammed's escape from Mecca, to which he later returned and conquered.

Mecca is one of Saudi Arabia's two federal capitals and it annually attracts as many as 15 million people of the Islam faith, known as Muslims. All Muslims are required to make a pilgrimage, or *hajj*, to the holy city at least once in their lifetime. If they die en route, they are considered martyrs. Martyrdoms are relatively common because of the severe climate and rough terrain frequently encountered during the pilgrimage. It has taken some pedestrian pilgrims from Asia as long as three years to arrive in Mecca.

The most significant shrine in the holy city is a black granite temple situated in the courtyard of the great mosque, El Haram. The temple is shaped like a cube, with each side measuring approximately 40 feet. In one corner of the temple is the Kaaba stone, presumably given to Abraham by the angel Gabriel. Every pilgrim is required to kiss the stone, which has become hollowed out by centuries of prayerful obligation. Over time, the temple has been destroyed by fires, floods, and other natural calamities, but it has always been rebuilt at the same site.

The pilgrimage rites, originated by Mohammed, have changed little since the seventh century. Pilgrims are still required to wear special garments and to remain bareheaded during the first days of their pilgrimage. They must also walk the circumference of the temple seven times, followed by seven circuits of a course between nearby holy hills. Throughout the pilgrimage, believers must refrain from hunting, killing, personal adornment, and sexual intercourse. When a Muslim has completed all of these rituals, he has earned the honored title of "pilgrim."

The religion of Islam is popular, with over 500 million practicing Muslims worldwide. Along with making a pilgrimage to Mecca, faithful Muslims must confess daily, give alms, and fast through the daylight hours of the holy month of Ramadan. They must also pray five times daily, at dawn, noon, mid-afternoon, dusk, and at night. Prayers are always made with the head bowed to the ground out of respect for Allah. And the believer must also face in the direction of Mecca—the city that embodies the tradition and the spirituality of Islam.

Recalling Facts

1. Mecca is located in
   - ☐ a. Iran.
   - ☐ b. Islam.
   - ☐ c. Saudi Arabia.

2. The founder of Islam was
   - ☐ a. Abraham.
   - ☐ b. Mohammed.
   - ☐ c. Gabriel.

3. Those practicing the Islamic faith number approximately
   - ☐ a. 15 million.
   - ☐ b. 200 million.
   - ☐ c. 500 million.

4. "Hajj" is the Arabic word for
   - ☐ a. pilgrimage.
   - ☐ b. martyrdom.
   - ☐ c. God.

5. Muslims must make a pilgrimage to Mecca
   - ☐ a. once in a lifetime.
   - ☐ b. once every five years.
   - ☐ c. five times in a lifetime.

Understanding the Passage

6. Mecca is the holiest city in the Islamic faith, in part because it's the
   - ☐ a. oldest city in the Middle East.
   - ☐ b. site of Abraham's death.
   - ☐ c. birthplace of Mohammed.

7. Martyrdoms sometimes occur during pilgrimages because
   - ☐ a. the Middle East is a violent and turbulent area.
   - ☐ b. pilgrims encounter severe climate and rough terrain.
   - ☐ c. sacrifice is an important element of the Islamic faith.

8. The author states that the rites of pilgrimage
   - ☐ a. have changed little since their origin.
   - ☐ b. are based on pagan practices.
   - ☐ c. are practiced by female Muslims only.

9. When Muslims pray, they bow their heads to the ground because
   - ☐ a. they are closer to Mecca in that position.
   - ☐ b. it shows respect to Allah.
   - ☐ c. the earth is considered holy.

10. We can infer that the Islamic faith
   - ☐ a. has many time-honored traditions.
   - ☐ b. is practiced by many, but respected by few.
   - ☐ c. is the oldest religion.

11 The Cast of the Operating Room

The surgeon stands in the spotlight, but the real stars of every operation are the supporting cast. Before the physician lifts the first instrument, an array of workers have been hard at work setting the stage for surgery.

Laboratory technicians run tests on the patient's blood prior to surgery to ensure the patient is in optimal condition for an operation. Blood bank technicians prepare blood for transfusion, in case it's needed during surgery. Laundry workers wash and iron linens, gowns, drapes, and scrub suits—crucial gear for even the smallest procedure in the operating room (O.R.). Supply workers ensure that there are enough surgical instruments for every contingency in the O.R. They also make sure that all the tools are in proper working order.

No operation could be performed without the hospital's pharmacy. It is the pharmacy's responsibility to prepare the drugs and anesthetic agents that are essential to the patient's safety and comfort.

Closer to the operation, orderlies play a key role in keeping the patient at ease during the transition from hospital room to operating room. Orderlies bring patients to the O.R. and position them on the operating table.

Once the patient is in place in the O.R., the anesthetist prepares to sedate the patient. The anesthetist relaxes the patient, while administering the drugs that allow the surgeon to begin the operation.

The stage manager of the operation is the circulating nurse, who must make certain that everyone in the O.R. is functioning properly. This nurse must also ensure that every instrument that might be needed is on hand and ready for the surgeon to use.

Manual dexterity is crucial to the job of the scrub technician. It is this worker's job to hand the instruments to the surgeon throughout the course of the operation.

When the operation is over, the supporting cast is still on the job. Laboratory pathologists analyze specimens provided from the operation. They work to unravel the mystery of a patient's illness, uncovering the location and extent of disease. The pathologists' efforts help physicians determine the course of the patient's convalescence and recovery.

The last link in the chain of the supporting cast is the recovery room nurse. It is this nurse's job to monitor the patient's condition following surgery and to catch and prevent any potential complications. The recovery room nurse also gets to deliver the closing lines, "The operation is over. You're going to be fine."

Reading Time_____ Comprehension Score_____ Words per Minute_____

Recalling Facts

1. Patient blood tests are run by
   □ a. laboratory technicians.
   □ b. blood bank technicians.
   □ c. pharmacy technicians.

2. O.R. stands for
   □ a. orderly recovery.
   □ b. operating room.
   □ c. operation recovery.

3. The pharmacy is responsible for
   □ a. supplying blood.
   □ b. administering drugs.
   □ c. preparing anesthetics.

4. Orderlies are responsible for
   □ a. maintaining quiet in the operating room.
   □ b. positioning the patient on the operating table.
   □ c. sterilizing the surgical instruments.

5. The scrub technician
   □ a. hands the surgeon instruments.
   □ b. washes the surgeon's hands.
   □ c. scrubs the patient.

Understanding the Passage

6. The person most responsible for the smooth running of the operating room is the
   □ a. anesthetist.
   □ b. circulating nurse.
   □ c. scrub nurse.

7. The author implies that all surgery requires
   □ a. lots of money.
   □ b. complex equipment.
   □ c. a team effort.

8. The person most likely to be credited with a successful operation is the
   □ a. surgeon.
   □ b. patient.
   □ c. head nurse.

9. Blood bank technicians always prepare blood for transfusions because
   □ a. it enables them to run tests on the patient.
   □ b. a patient might need it during surgery.
   □ c. transfusions are routine surgical procedures.

10. We can infer that the person most likely to learn the precise cause of a patient's illness is the
    □ a. laboratory pathologist.
    □ b. surgeon.
    □ c. anesthetist.

The Cost of Civilization

It didn't happen overnight. The problem of polluted air has been festering for centuries.

Suddenly the problem of air pollution is becoming critical and is erupting right before our eyes. Not only do our eyes burn as they focus through murky air, but when the air clears, we see trees and vegetation dying. We must realize that this destruction can no longer be pinned to some mysterious cause. The one major culprit is air pollution.

Today's air pollution is an unfortunate by-product of the growth of civilization. Civilized man desires goods that require heavy industrialization and mass production. Machines and factories sometimes pollute and taint the air with substances that are dangerous to man and the environment. These substances include radioactive dust, salt spray, herbicide and pesticide aerosols, liquid droplets of acidic matter, gases, and sometimes soil particles. These materials can act alone to irritate objects and forms of life. More dangerously, they join together to act upon the environment. Only lately have we begun recognizing some of their dangerous consequences.

Scientists have not yet been able to obtain a complete report on the effects of air pollution on trees. They do know, however, that sulfur dioxide, fluorides, and ozone destroy trees and that individual trees respond differently to the numerous particulate and gaseous pollutants. Sometimes trees growing in a single area under attack by pollutants will show symptoms of injury or will die while their neighbors remain healthy. Scientists believe this difference in response depends on the kind of tree and its genetic makeup. Other factors, such as the tree's stage of growth and nearness to the pollution source, the amount of pollutant, and the length of the pollution attack also play a part. In short, whether or not a tree dies as a result of air pollution depends on a combination of host and environmental factors.

For the most part, air pollutants injure trees. To conifers, which have year-round needles, air pollution causes early balding. In this event, trees cannot maintain normal food production levels. Undernourished and weakened, they are open to attack by a host of insects, diseases, and other environmental stresses. Death often follows.

Air pollution may also cause hardwoods to lose their leaves. Because their leaves are borne only for a portion of the year and are replaced the following year, air pollution injury to hardwoods may not be so severe.

Recalling Facts

1. The author attributes today's air pollution to
   - ☐ a. man's carelessness.
   - ☐ b. the growth of civilization.
   - ☐ c. environmental imbalance.

2. One of the chemicals that can destroy trees is
   - ☐ a. carbon monoxide.
   - ☐ b. fluoride.
   - ☐ c. potassium nitrate.

3. The resistance of some trees to disease can be traced to
   - ☐ a. genetic makeup.
   - ☐ b. protective foliage.
   - ☐ c. thick bark.

4. Air pollution first attacks the tree's
   - ☐ a. sap.
   - ☐ b. roots.
   - ☐ c. foliage.

5. Air pollution causes the most damage to
   - ☐ a. hardwoods.
   - ☐ b. conifers.
   - ☐ c. fruit trees.

Understanding the Passage

6. The author suggests that we are aware of pollution today because
   - ☐ a. records show the seriousness of pollution over the years.
   - ☐ b. laboratory tests have proved that chemicals are pollutants.
   - ☐ c. we can see signs of it all around us.

7. The author implies that the greatest source of pollution is
   - ☐ a. heavy industry.
   - ☐ b. chemical processing plants.
   - ☐ c. urban expansion.

8. The author points out that conifers
   - ☐ a. grow best in temperate climates.
   - ☐ b. have needles instead of leaves.
   - ☐ c. have been studied more extensively than hardwoods.

9. The reader can assume that
   - ☐ a. trees respond differently to pollution.
   - ☐ b. some trees can be cured of pollution disease.
   - ☐ c. air pollution is most serious in city areas.

10. We can conclude that
   - ☐ a. air pollution is easier to control than water pollution.
   - ☐ b. research on the effects of air pollution is incomplete.
   - ☐ c. the impact of air pollution has been known for centuries.

13 The King of Ragtime

Scott Joplin, born into a musical family in Texarkana, Texas in 1868, was destined to become one of America's greatest black artists. At the age of 14, he had mastered the piano and was determined to become a professional musician. Young Joplin left home and headed for Missouri where he would begin his legendary career as the self-proclaimed "King of the Ragtime Composers."

While in Missouri, Joplin worked in cafes, brothels, saloons, and steamboats that sailed the Mississippi. He was exposed to a wide array of musical styles and became intrigued with a new kind of music called "ragged time," which featured syncopated rhythms. The music which came to be known as "ragtime" failed to achieve broad approval in its era both because of its link with brothels and because it was developed by itinerant black pianists. However, this lack of respectability gave ragtime a kind of underground popularity.

Scott Joplin had become the leading ragtime musician by the time he was 28. But despite his fame, he wanted more. Joplin began studying music at George Smith College in Sedalia, Missouri. He worked at putting ragtime into writing by learning formal musical notation.

Joplin supported himself by playing in bars, most notably, Will and Walker Williams' Maple Leaf Club, which was a breeding ground for the best musicians in the area. As a tribute to his employers, Joplin wrote "The Maple Leaf Rag," a piece he felt certain would earn him a national reputation. Within three years, Joplin had found a publisher, and "The Maple Leaf Rag" became an unqualified nationwide success.

With the money he earned from his hit song, Joplin moved to St. Louis to devote his career entirely to composing. The artist saw in ragtime a serious art form, comparable to the works of Europe's classical composers. Joplin wrote a ragtime ballet and opera, but his efforts failed. He consequently lost much of his money and was forced to return to the saloon circuit.

Nonetheless, Joplin persevered with his vision. He wrote another ragtime opera, a work he considered to be his masterpiece. But this effort too was doomed to failure. The disappointments of these unsuccessful creative efforts led Joplin to a nervous breakdown. He was committed to a mental institution, where he died in 1917.

Though Joplin died with a broken spirit, his music thrives today with a syncopated energy that is living proof of his musical genius.

Recalling Facts

1. Joplin was born in
   □ a. Texas.
   □ b. Missouri.
   □ c. Mississippi.

2. Joplin began his career as a
   □ a. ragtime composer.
   □ b. piano repairman.
   □ c. saloon pianist.

3. Joplin was named "King of the Ragtime Composers" by
   □ a. Walker Williams.
   □ b. George Smith.
   □ c. himself.

4. Ragtime is a musical style characterized by
   □ a. bright melodies.
   □ b. somber ballads.
   □ c. syncopated rhythms.

5. Joplin died in
   □ a. a brothel.
   □ b. a mental institution.
   □ c. his home.

Understanding the Passage

6. Ragtime lacked respectability because
   □ a. it was developed by itinerant black pianists.
   □ b. its lyrics were controversial.
   □ c. popular music was considered sinful.

7. Joplin wrote "The Maple Leaf Rag" because he
   □ a. thought it would make him wealthy.
   □ b. wanted to pay tribute to his employers.
   □ c. was nostalgic for the maple trees of his boyhood.

8. Joplin moved to St. Louis to
   □ a. study music in college.
   □ b. devote his career to composing.
   □ c. begin his career as a pianist.

9. The Maple Leaf Club was important because
   □ a. it was a breeding ground for talented musicians.
   □ b. its brothel was a leading tourist attraction.
   □ c. it was where Joplin was first employed.

10. The author implies Joplin's greatest musical contribution was as a
   □ a. ragtime composer.
   □ b. pianist.
   □ c. opera composer.

Cats' Eyes

What do cats' eyes and highway reflector signs have in common? They both act as retroreflectors.

Almost everyone has noticed the eerie, frightening appearance of animals at night, as their eyes seem to glow in reflected light. One may speculate that just as reflective highway signs alert the motorist to many road hazards, so early man was often warned of danger by light from his campfire reflected in the eyes of lurking predators. In both cases, the light is retroreflected, giving it a particularly bright appearance.

The principles of retroreflection have been understood for centuries. However, it has only been within the last sixty or seventy years, with the widespread use of the automobile, that this area of optics has received important commercial application. Today, there are many uses for retroreflective materials. They are purchased in very large quantities by government agencies for use on highways. They are applied to bicycles and motor vehicles to make them more visible at night. And they assist pilots by improving the visibility of runway markers.

Some uses for retroreflective materials are not related to safety. For example, these materials play a key role in helping railroads locate and make maximum use of their rolling stock. Color-coded retroreflective numerals, strips, or dots applied to the side of railway cars identify the cars by their individual inventory numbers and by the particular type of car. Optical scanners "read" and record this information as the train passes by, thus making it possible for railroad management to locate an individual car or to determine the distribution of boxcars throughout the rail network.

Large sums are spent on retroreflective materials, but purchasers have often had trouble deciding which specific materials will give the optimal performance. Performance is of concern not only from the standpoint of the brightness of reflected light, but also from the standpoint of its color. It is important, for example, that the yellow hues used in warning signals be of consistent color quality on all road signs so the driver can rely on color, as well as shape, to discern the signs' meanings.

Seven colors—silver, blue, yellow, red, green, brown, and orange—are currently used for marking the interstate highway system. Since 1971, the National Bureau of Standards has been working to develop instrumental test methods that could be used to evaluate the performance of retroreflective materials and to aid in the preparation of specifications for their purchase.

---

*Reading Time*_____ *Comprehension Score*_____ *Words per Minute*_____   **41**

Recalling Facts

1. Retroreflective materials are used
   - ☐ a. on planes.
   - ☐ b. on runways.
   - ☐ c. in terminals.

2. Retroreflective materials have been used extensively since the invention of
   - ☐ a. the automobile.
   - ☐ b. the laser beam.
   - ☐ c. photography.

3. Optical scanners are used by
   - ☐ a. some railroads.
   - ☐ b. many opticians.
   - ☐ c. computer scientists.

4. Which retroreflective color is not used on interstate highways?
   - ☐ a. silver
   - ☐ b. purple
   - ☐ c. brown

5. The National Bureau of Standards began work on retroreflective devices in
   - ☐ a. 1955.
   - ☐ b. 1963.
   - ☐ c. 1971.

Understanding the Passage

6. This article is primarily concerned with
   - ☐ a. technology in photoelectric cells.
   - ☐ b. retroreflection and tropism in animals and insects.
   - ☐ c. natural and man-made retroreflection.

7. The word predator is used to mean
   - ☐ a. scavenger.
   - ☐ b. wild animal.
   - ☐ c. evil person.

8. An optical scanner is probably a
   - ☐ a. mechanical device.
   - ☐ b. simple camera.
   - ☐ c. type of computer.

9. The article suggests that
   - ☐ a. government scientists are developing inexpensive retroreflectors.
   - ☐ b. the government manufactures retroreflective devices.
   - ☐ c. the government buys retroreflective devices from private companies.

10. The reader can conclude that
    - ☐ a. the use of retroreflective material is becoming greater each year.
    - ☐ b. retroreflective paint can be purchased at most hardware stores.
    - ☐ c. retroreflective materials give off light in the dark.

Egyptian pyramids were the dominant structures within building complexes which were built to cater to the needs of royalty and other notables after death. There are two types of pyramid construction: true pyramids, in which the sides slope continuously from the base to the summit, and step pyramids, in which all four sides are built in steps from the bottom to the top. Step pyramids are older—the first was built for King Zoser of the Third Dynasty in 2660 B.C. by the architect Imhotep. True pyramids superseded step pyramids in the Fourth Dynasty and were built for the next ten centuries.

Three important concerns governed the choice of a site for the construction of a pyramid. It had to be located near the royal residence, on the west bank of the Nile but out of reach of the annual floods, and at a place where the desert sands or rock were firm.

Pyramids which have been damaged often allow an analysis of their composition, demonstrating that the inner core of most pyramids was built in upright layers around a central nucleus. Each layer consisted of horizontal courses of local stone with an outer facade of fine limestone from the Tura quarries in the Maqattan Hills near Giza. The outer sides of the nucleus and of the surrounding layers inclined inward at an angle of 75° which served to counteract the tendency of the masonry to yield to outward pressure. If they were located within the structure, corridors and chambers were built as the monument was being erected, while subterranean corridors and chambers were tunnelled in the rock before any masonry was laid.

At the same time as the core was being constructed, the entire pyramid was encased with a facade of Tura limestone. Before insertion, each casing block was cut to the pyramid angle of about 52°. Although Egyptian mathematical texts give no evidence that the nature of π was understood, the Great Pyramid slopes at an angle of 51° 51' which resulted from making the height equal to the radius of a circle whose circumference was equal to the perimeter of the pyramid's base. The last stone block to be put in place—the capstone—was a miniature facsimile of the pyramid, usually of granite. It was secured in place by a tenon projecting from its base which fitted into a socket within the top course of limestone masonry.

Recalling Facts

1. The sides of true pyramids have
   - ☐ a. a slope of 45°.
   - ☐ b. steps.
   - ☐ c. continuous slopes.

2. The sides of step pyramids have
   - ☐ a. a slope of 45°.
   - ☐ b. steps.
   - ☐ c. continuous slopes.

3. The outer sides of the pyramid nucleus inclined inward at a
   - ☐ a. 75° angle.
   - ☐ b. 52° angle.
   - ☐ c. 45° angle.

4. The outer facade was often constructed of
   - ☐ a. granite.
   - ☐ b. sandstone.
   - ☐ c. limestone.

5. The capstone was often constructed of
   - ☐ a. granite.
   - ☐ b. sandstone.
   - ☐ c. limestone.

Understanding the Passage

6. Limestone blocks for the pyramids were quarried in
   - ☐ a. Egypt.
   - ☐ b. North Africa.
   - ☐ c. the Far East.

7. The site chosen for a pyramid had to be near the
   - ☐ a. Nile delta.
   - ☐ b. royal residence.
   - ☐ c. other pyramids.

8. The Egyptian Imhotep was a famous
   - ☐ a. court musician.
   - ☐ b. pharaoh.
   - ☐ c. pyramid architect.

9. It can be established that the 51° 51′ slope of the Great Pyramid
   - ☐ a. was an accidental choice of measurement.
   - ☐ b. was a planned choice of measurement.
   - ☐ c. resulted from a mathematical equation for π.

10. Inner rooms and corridors of pyramids were constructed
    - ☐ a. after the core.
    - ☐ b. before the core.
    - ☐ c. at the same time as the core.

16 Counting the World's Population

Almost since the beginning of mankind, governments have been recording the numbers of their populace. The first known census report took place in 3800 B.C. in Babylonia for the purpose of deciding who should pay taxes. As time went by, governments found other, more creative uses for knowing their numbers. Egyptian King Ramses II used the census not only to determine who should pay taxes, but also to figure out how to divide land for farming and to decide who could provide manpower for various government projects. These new ideas came about in the mid-1200s—B.C.

William the Conqueror brought the concept of census taking to England in 1085. All landowners were required to name their holdings for the purpose of taxation. By the fifteenth century, Tudor kings found a new twist to the Egyptians' use of the census. They too used the population count as a means of getting ready manpower for important government projects—namely, replenishing troops in the ongoing battles in western Europe.

A rebellious tide swept over England, however, in the mid-1700s. A bill to authorize a regular census was defeated in Parliament on the grounds that it would give valuable information to England's enemies. But the tide of rebellion soon turned, and in 1800 England established its first regular census.

Meanwhile the United States had already had an ongoing census for ten years. It was authorized in the Constitution for the purpose of deciding how many members of Congress would be needed for a fair representation of the American people. The constitutional article also established that the census would be taken in 1790 and every ten years thereafter. And so it has.

Since its beginning, the American census has gone through many changes. Today the census provides more than a count of the people who live here. It takes polls on transportation, economic planning, and agriculture. The census also provides data for most government agency statistics, such as the unemployment rate.

The census is taken very seriously in the United States. It is illegal to willfully refuse to provide information to census takers. Non-compliers are handed either a jail term or a fine.

Counting costs have risen since 1790. The government spent about a penny per person to count post-Revolutionary Americans. Today the census costs $250 million—more than a dollar per person. That's a long way since 3800 B.C.

Recalling Facts

1. The first known census report took place in Babylonia in
   - a. 1085.
   - b. 1200 B.C.
   - c. 3800 B.C.

2. The first census was created for the sole purpose of
   - a. counting available troops.
   - b. taxing the populace.
   - c. dividing farmland.

3. The concept of census taking was brought to England by
   - a. William the Conqueror.
   - b. King Ramses II.
   - c. the United States Constitution.

4. The census was used as a means of providing military strength by
   - a. King Ramses II.
   - b. Tudor kings.
   - c. William the Conqueror.

5. The American census today costs the government approximately
   - a. $.01/person.
   - b. $.10/person.
   - c. $1.00/person.

Understanding the Passage

6. Parliament defeated a bill authorizing a regular census because it
   - a. would give England's enemies cause for rebellion.
   - b. might give valuable information to England's enemies.
   - c. would be too expensive.

7. The United States first authorized a census for the purpose of
   - a. completing the Constitution.
   - b. determining Congressional representation.
   - c. taxing the citizenry.

8. We can infer that census taking is
   - a. an ancient practice.
   - b. a recent political development.
   - c. an efficient means of taxation.

9. King Ramses II's contribution to the history of the census was
   - a. introducing census taking to England.
   - b. making it the foundation of a broad-based tax structure.
   - c. using it to identify manpower for government projects.

10. The author implies the American census is
    - a. relatively inexpensive to conduct.
    - b. an exact count of the citizenry.
    - c. important to various government branches.

17 Where Do All the Wild Birds Go?

The National Wildlife Refuge System is still growing. The Department of the Interior recognizes that a secure habitat for many kinds of wildlife is far from adequate. Many more acres of wetlands, marshes, swamps, lakes, and streams must be added to the present chain of refuges if water-loving species are to survive as a basic resource. New areas are needed to provide a habitat for birds and other mammals in danger of extinction.

Although national refuges protect many types of wildlife, they play an especially important role in management of the international migratory waterfowl. Three-fourths of all refuges were established originally for these birds. Since 1934, most of the money used to purchase waterfowl refuges has come from the sale of migratory bird stamps.

Within the National Wildlife Refuge System are also numerous waterfowl production areas. These are small pothole marshes in the prairie states capable of producing large numbers of ducks. Emphasis has been placed on the acquisition of these areas to prevent their imminent destruction by drainage and conversion to non-wildlife uses. Over a million acres of these small but valuable wetlands have been purchased and leased.

National wildlife refuges are popular as places to find large numbers of many kinds of wildlife. Few other sites afford opportunities to see such great concentrations of waterfowl and other birds. More than 25 refuges can claim gatherings in excess of 50,000 wild geese. Refuges not only harbor birds and mammals, but also provide for species of plants, insects, amphibians, and reptiles that each year become more difficult to find in other places. Many refuges have fine scenic and historical values that are preserved along with the wildlife.

Our national wildlife refuges are often thought of as self-operating wildlife paradises from the time they are established. More often than not, they have been developed from areas misused in the past by drainage, lumbering, burning, and overgrazing and need restoration to become a first-class wildlife habitat. This is accomplished mainly with dams, dikes, and fences and through farming programs to produce special and supplemental wildlife foods. Management may also employ irrigation systems, soil conservation practices, or forestry programs.

Many refuges contribute substantially to local economies. By law, local governments share in the revenues from grazing, haying, sale of timber, and other economic uses on refuges necessary for the best management of the wildlife habitat. The economic benefits that humans receive coincide with the preservation benefits for the waterfowl.

Recalling Facts

1. The National Wildlife Refuge System is a branch of the Department of
   - ☐ a. State.
   - ☐ b. Commerce.
   - ☐ c. the Interior.

2. Wildlife refuges are especially important to
   - ☐ a. nesting birds.
   - ☐ b. tropical species.
   - ☐ c. migratory waterfowl.

3. Money used to purchase wildlife refuges is raised through
   - ☐ a. coin auctions.
   - ☐ b. hunting permits.
   - ☐ c. stamp sales.

4. How many refuges have bird populations in excess of 50,000?
   - ☐ a. twenty-five
   - ☐ b. fifty
   - ☐ c. seventy-five

5. Refuges are usually developed from
   - ☐ a. virgin territory.
   - ☐ b. donated lands.
   - ☐ c. misused lands.

Understanding the Passage

6. The author implies that many of the birds in refuges
   - ☐ a. are killed by hunters annually.
   - ☐ b. are threatened with extinction.
   - ☐ c. prefer living in salt water marshes.

7. The author states that pothole marshes are
   - ☐ a. used as breeding grounds.
   - ☐ b. often expanded into large swamps.
   - ☐ c. set aside as hunting areas.

8. A large number of pothole marshes are located
   - ☐ a. in the plains states.
   - ☐ b. along the Atlantic Coast.
   - ☐ c. in the Southwest.

9. Pothole marshes are
   - ☐ a. dangerous sandtraps.
   - ☐ b. small, valuable swamps.
   - ☐ c. deep, grass-covered quagmires.

10. Birds and animals in wildlife refuges are fed with
    - ☐ a. government surplus food.
    - ☐ b. food donated by concerned citizens.
    - ☐ c. food grown in refuge areas.

King Tut

Tutankhamen is one of history's most famous pharaohs, not because of his skills as a political leader, but primarily because of the splendor of his grave. Tut became Egypt's pharaoh at the age of 10, and ruled for nine years from 1361–1352 B.C. Though his rule was brief and unremarkable, his grave furnishings are considered among the world's finest examples of Egyptian burial practices.

Few Egyptian royal burial sites have survived because of many centuries of rampant pillaging. At one time, pyramids were the most popular grave sites of Egyptian rulers. But not one pyramid escaped the hands of ancient tomb robbers. Consequently, Egyptian leaders abandoned the practice of pyramid burial and began carving royal tombs out of the face of the Nile cliffs. Nonetheless, by the 11th century B.C., no royal tombs were left intact.

Historians suggest that Tutankhamen's tomb survived by accident. It is said that the tomb's small size and the insignificance of its occupant kept it relatively free of robbery attempts. Thieves did try to rob Tutankhamen's grave shortly after his entombment, but evidence shows that they were caught. Most of the stolen goods were returned, and the grave was never pillaged again.

Two hundred years after Tutankhamen's death, preparations were made for the burial of King Ramses VI. The tomb's architects chose to build the grave in the cliffs above Tutankhamen's burial site. As work got under way on the new tomb, grave workers discarded their unused limestone down the cliff. The stone rested atop Tut's grave, completely covering it and providing an effective sealant. Tutankhamen's tomb remained covered for almost 3,000 years.

The tomb was discovered by British archaeologist Lord Carnarvon and his American assistant Howard Carter on November 4, 1922, when the steps leading down into the tomb were uncovered. It took the expeditioners eight years to excavate and preserve the tomb. The task was particularly difficult because they could see only by candlelight and were limited to working between the months of October to April.

Nearly all of the ancient ruler's tomb now resides in the National Museum of Cairo. Tutankhamen's body still lies in the stone sarcophagus, which has never been replaced, and the ruler's outer coffin is wrought entirely of gold. The monetary value of this important archaeological find is incalculable. But it is certain that the tomb's historical worth is of far greater significance than the reign of the youthful Tutankhamen.

Recalling Facts

1. Tutankhamen became Egypt's pharaoh at the age of
   - ☐ a. 10.
   - ☐ b. 21.
   - ☐ c. 30.

2. Tutankhamen reigned during the
   - ☐ a. 12th century B.C.
   - ☐ b. 13th century B.C.
   - ☐ c. 14th century B.C.

3. Pyramids were used as
   - ☐ a. places of worship.
   - ☐ b. burial grounds.
   - ☐ c. royal palaces.

4. King Tut's tomb was discovered in
   - ☐ a. 1822.
   - ☐ b. 1882.
   - ☐ c. 1922.

5. Tutankhamen's burial furnishings belong to the
   - ☐ a. British Lord Carnarvon.
   - ☐ b. National Museum of Cairo.
   - ☐ c. the Egyptian royal family.

Understanding the Passage

6. The author states that Tutankhamen was most famous for his
   - ☐ a. political effectiveness.
   - ☐ b. grave furnishings.
   - ☐ c. military genius.

7. Royal tombs were carved out of the Nile cliffs
   - ☐ a. because of Egyptian religious beliefs.
   - ☐ b. to fend off grave robbers.
   - ☐ c. for longterm grave preservation.

8. Tutankhamen's tomb remained relatively free of robbery attempts because
   - ☐ a. of its occupant's insignificance.
   - ☐ b. King Ramses guards protected it.
   - ☐ c. it was in a secret location.

9. The task of uncovering Tut's grave was difficult because
   - ☐ a. of Egyptian laws protecting royal graves.
   - ☐ b. the site was steep and dangerous.
   - ☐ c. the archaeologists could work only half the year.

10. We can infer that few Egyptian royal graves survive because
    - ☐ a. most of them deteriorated over time.
    - ☐ b. most were robbed of their furnishings.
    - ☐ c. their location is a long lost secret.

19   A Long-Forgotten Weapon

For more than 2,000 years before the appearance of Greek Fire in the seventh century, incendiary weapons had been used in combat situations. For example, incendiaries had been deployed by the Persian and Assyrian armies and primarily consisted of some type of flammable material, such as pitch or naptha, placed in a container and hurled at the enemy. But Greek Fire, which consisted of a stream of burning oil expelled under pressure with a force similar to a modern flame-thrower, was a great "improvement" on these earlier weapons. It was regarded with considerable apprehension by those who did not possess its secret and was developed to be used on land and sea by the Byzantines, who were the medieval successors to the Eastern Roman Empire.

Although many scientists and historians have attempted to discover the secret of Greek Fire, the mistaken medieval belief that the secret was in its chemical composition has hampered this research. It is evident that many Byzantines were not aware of how the device really worked and for a good reason, since it was a carefully-kept state secret.

The medieval sources distinguish three main components for this inflammatory weapon: a pump, a swivel tub, and a brazier. It is known that the material projected was crude oil procured from regions northeast of the Black Sea. The oil may have been distilled, although the process was not widely known in the seventh century. The principle of the Greek Fire must have rested in preheating the oil, which was then placed in a sealed bronze container, increasing flammability and reducing the thickness of the oil. When adequate pressure had been produced, both by heating the oil and by using the pump, a tap or valve was opened and the oil was forced out under tremendous pressure through the swivel tub where it was then ignited. The brazier, or heating device, consisted not of an open wood fire which would have been dangerous on a ship, but of a "slow match" of smoldering cloth, which was brought rapidly up to the required temperature with bellows.

Whatever the precise details of this weapon, it seems plausible that the Greek Fire projector worked in roughly this manner and can be considered an early Molotov Cocktail which hurled burning oil onto enemy ships and troops with great violence. Greek Fire may be said to be an early example of "man's inhumanity to man."

Recalling Facts

1. A component of Greek Fire was probably
   - ☐ a. oil.
   - ☐ b. gunpowder.
   - ☐ c. pitch.

2. Medieval researchers believed that the secret of Greek Fire was in its
   - ☐ a. design.
   - ☐ b. chemical composition.
   - ☐ c. mechanics.

3. The Byzantine Empire was the medieval descendant of the
   - ☐ a. Roman Empire.
   - ☐ b. Greek states.
   - ☐ c. Assyrian Empire.

4. A Molotov Cocktail is a
   - ☐ a. hot beverage.
   - ☐ b. modern weapon.
   - ☐ c. Russian missile.

5. Flammable materials used in early warfare were
   - ☐ a. pitch and naptha.
   - ☐ b. oil and pitch.
   - ☐ c. poisonous gases.

Understanding the Passage

6. The mechanics of Greek Fire were generally unknown because
   - ☐ a. medieval sources thought the secret was in its chemical makeup.
   - ☐ b. it was a state secret.
   - ☐ c. it was greatly feared by armies of the seventh century.

7. The crude oil used in Greek Fire was
   - ☐ a. not distilled.
   - ☐ b. perhaps distilled.
   - ☐ c. always distilled.

8. A brazier, used to make Greek Fire, was a
   - ☐ a. pumping device.
   - ☐ b. heating device.
   - ☐ c. projection device.

9. Preheating the oil served to
   - ☐ a. increase its thickness.
   - ☐ b. decrease its flammability.
   - ☐ c. increase its flammability.

10. A swivel tub functioned as an apparatus to
    - ☐ a. ignite the preheated oil.
    - ☐ b. cool down the preheated oil.
    - ☐ c. eject the preheated oil.

20 Chocolate: Everyone's Favorite Sweet

The Aztecs of Mexico are known to have made a beverage from cocoa beans, honey, maize, vanilla, and spices which they called "chocolatl." On his fourth voyage to the Americas in 1502, Columbus took cocoa beans back to Spain. The Spaniards improved the taste with the addition of sugar, and chocolate eventually became a popular and expensive drink among European aristocrats. In 1728, Dr. Joseph Fry constructed the first chocolate factory, and one hundred years later the Dutchman Van Houten patented a machine for pressing cocoa powder. This made feasible modern dark chocolate which is solid chocolate made of the ground cocoa bean, cocoa butter, and sugar. In the case of milk chocolate, milk or dried milk is also an ingredient.

To make chocolate, a carefully blended selection of beans are first cleaned and mixed. After cleaning, the beans are roasted to bring out their full flavor; both the temperature and length of roasting critically determine the flavor.

The next part of the process is winnowing the beans, where the object is to separate the "nib," or inside of the bean from the shell or husk. Various machines are designed for this, some of which will extract a greater proportion of the nibs. After the nibs have been broken into small fragments, they are ground into a soft mass from which all chocolate products are made.

The chocolate mass is then mixed with fine sugar and additional cocoa butter; the latter is produced by pressing some of the cocoa mass, leaving cocoa cake as a residue which is manufactured into cocoa powder. In the case of milk chocolate, milk is also added at this time. Excess acids and moisture are extracted and the mixture is refined, which involves passing it through rollers until the proper particle size is reached. This important step determines the texture of the chocolate.

The next step in the process is "conching" which is an art that chocolatiers have disageed about since chocolate was first invented. This consists of kneading the chocolate over a shell or conch-shaped roller, and of aeration and temperature treatment, during which the product acquires a complete uniformity, and creaminess. At this stage, the flavor is fully developed. The length of the conching time and temperature is a secret of the chocolatier, but it is usually ten to twenty-four hours at 65°C for milk chocolate and twenty-four to ninety-six hours at 75°C for dark chocolate.

Recalling Facts

1. What group of native Americans first used chocolate?
   - ☐ a. the Aztecs
   - ☐ b. the Incas
   - ☐ c. the Navajo

2. "Chocolatl" was an Aztec
   - ☐ a. monument.
   - ☐ b. beverage.
   - ☐ c. ruler.

3. What is the different ingredient between dark and milk chocolate?
   - ☐ a. sugar
   - ☐ b. milk
   - ☐ c. cocoa butter

4. What part of the cocoa bean is the nib?
   - ☐ a. the shell
   - ☐ b. the inside
   - ☐ c. the entire bean

5. Conching refers to the process of
   - ☐ a. collecting shells.
   - ☐ b. kneading chocolate.
   - ☐ c. winnowing cocoa.

Understanding the Passage

6. Chocolate was initially a drink for what group of Europeans?
   - ☐ a. the upper class
   - ☐ b. the peasants
   - ☐ c. all social classes

7. For texture, the most important stage in chocolate making is
   - ☐ a. winnowing the cocoa beans.
   - ☐ b. rolling the chocolate mass.
   - ☐ c. conching the chocolate mass.

8. For smoothness, the most important stage in chocolate making is
   - ☐ a. conching the chocolate mass.
   - ☐ b. winnowing the cocoa beans.
   - ☐ c. roasting the cocoa beans.

9. What stage of chocolate manufacture is a heavily guarded secret?
   - ☐ a. the winnowing stage
   - ☐ b. the packaging stage
   - ☐ c. the conching stage

10. A good title for this selection could be
    - ☐ a. A Diabetic's Nightmare.
    - ☐ b. A Dieter's Delight.
    - ☐ c. The Process of Chocolate Making.

21   Continental Summers

North American summers are hot. As the advancing sun drives back the polar air, the land is opened up to light and solar heat and occupied by masses of moist, warm air spun landward off the tropical ocean. With these rain-filled visitors come the tongues of dry desert air that flock northward out of Mexico and, occasionally, the hot winds that howl down the Rockies' eastern slopes.

Inequalities of atmospheric heating and cooling, of moistness and aridity, are regulated at middle latitudes by horizontal and vertical mixing. The mixing apparatus is the parade of cyclones, low-pressure centers, and anticyclones, which lie at the heart of most weather, good and bad.

The cyclones and anticyclones drift in the mid-latitude westerlies, the prevailing eastward-blowing winds that follow a scalloped path around the northern hemisphere. The large-scale undulations of these winds may extend for thousands of miles and are called planetary waves. Their high-speed core is the jet stream, which snakes across the continent some six to eight miles up, keeping mainly to the cool side of highs and lows as they form, spin, and die below it.

The kind of weather predominating in an area over a period of time depends largely on the prevailing position and orientation of the jet stream. As the continent warms, the jet stream shifts northward, along with the tracks of surface weather disturbances. Cyclones bring June thundershowers to the Plains. The humid spring of Georgia becomes the muggy summer of Illinois. These alternations of instability, hot and cool, moist and dry, combine annually to generate the average summer climate for North America.

When these alternating processes are somehow interrupted, the climatic "norm" of summer is marred by a heat wave. The anomaly is usually associated with a change in the planetary waves, so that the prevailing winds from the southwestern deserts sweep farther north than usual and blanket a large region with hot, often humid, air at ground level. An upper-level high may settle over the mid-continent, destroying cloud cover with its descending, compression-heated currents, until the blessing of fair weather turns to the curse of drought. In addition, heat from the hot, dry ground feeds back into the atmosphere, tending to perpetuate the heat wave circulation.

Whatever the cause, the effect can be uncomfortable and dangerous, especially for the very young or old. Continental heat waves live in human memory the way fierce winters do.

Recalling Facts

1. North American summers are considered
   - ☐ a. mild.
   - ☐ b. cool.
   - ☐ c. hot.

2. As summer approaches, the sun drives back
   - ☐ a. arctic air masses.
   - ☐ b. polar air masses.
   - ☐ c. Pacific air masses.

3. The jet stream is usually found no higher than
   - ☐ a. 8 miles.
   - ☐ b. 125 miles.
   - ☐ c. 1,600 miles.

4. As summer approaches, the jet stream shifts
   - ☐ a. southward.
   - ☐ b. westward.
   - ☐ c. northward.

5. An anticyclone is actually a
   - ☐ a. low-pressure area.
   - ☐ b. high-pressure area.
   - ☐ c. cold front.

Understanding the Passage

6. The author implies that
   - ☐ a. there are two systems of weather—upper level and lower level.
   - ☐ b. the East coast is susceptible to hurricanes during summer.
   - ☐ c. cities are warmer at night than rural areas.

7. The author suggests that changes in climate are the result of
   - ☐ a. shifts in the movement of planetary waves.
   - ☐ b. advancing low-pressure areas.
   - ☐ c. stationary fronts.

8. The author describes the summer season using
   - ☐ a. allegory.
   - ☐ b. figurative language.
   - ☐ c. colloquial language.

9. The author discusses a weather anomaly in the form of
   - ☐ a. a heat wave.
   - ☐ b. an early snowfall.
   - ☐ c. unseasonable rainfall.

10. We can conclude that
    - ☐ a. the atmosphere is never stable.
    - ☐ b. tornados cannot be predicted accurately.
    - ☐ c. summer weather is more predictable than winter weather.

Container gardening is especially adapted to contemporary living. Houseplants are as compatible with the bold, simple lines of contemporary architecture as with the intricate lines of many older homes. Plants display great variety of form and texture. They can be used to create instant indoor gardens; they can be moved from one home to another; and they can be moved outdoors in the summer and indoors during the cooler months.

Space is not a problem. Container gardening can be conducted in a single pot on a table or windowsill, in a more elaborate room divider, or in a built-in planter. Just as there are many kinds of plants, there are many kinds of containers. The choice ranges from the common clay pot to cans, jars, boxes, baskets, and tubs. Most people select containers for both their practical and aesthetic qualities. These include cost, availability, weight, strength, durability, attractiveness, and decorative and sentimental value.

Particularly important considerations for good plant growth are the volume and depth of the container, and some provision for drainage. Containers should have drainage holes in the bottom, and a layer of pebbles or broken crockery above this. Watertight containers allow excess water to accumulate around the roots, causing them to rot. Furthermore, drainage holes give roots access to oxygen. The container should be large enough to allow growth; when the roots come through the bottom, it is time to transplant.

Besides the right kind of container, some fundamental requirements for plant growth must be provided. Plants need light, water, nutrients, and a satisfactory temperature range. Although the evaporation of water through the container walls is not critical, plants in porous containers will require more frequent watering to maintain moisture levels than will those in nonporous containers. Light is the most critical requirement. The levels of all the other requirements are adjusted in relation to the amount of light that plants receive. When plants don't have enough light, they grow slowly and become tall and spindly; it becomes difficult to avoid overwatering them. It is also important not to give plants too much light; a florist will know the optimal amount of light to give a plant.

In order to begin a home container garden, consult a gardening book, florist, or local greenhouse owner. Choose a plant with a reputation for health and easy manageability for your initial attempt at gardening.

You can get as involved as you wish with your plants. Some people keep terrariums because they require no care, while others play music for, or even talk to their plants. It's all up to the individual, and some plants are luckier than others!

Recalling Facts

1. With container gardening,
   plants are
   □ a. unhealthy.
   □ b. immoveable.
   □ c. portable.

2. The most critical requirement
   for plants is
   □ a. moisture.
   □ b. nutrients.
   □ c. light.

3. According to the author,
   some plants
   □ a. can be taken outdoors
        during warm weather.
   □ b. will produce larger blooms
        if they are given milk.
   □ c. need water daily.

4. A common material for
   flower pots is
   □ a. clay.
   □ b. fiberglass.
   □ c. plastic.

5. Plants in porous containers
   require extra
   □ a. sunlight.
   □ b. warmth.
   □ c. water.

Understanding the Passage

6. This article is primarily about
   □ a. caring for indoor plants.
   □ b. growing tropical plants.
   □ c. making containers for plants.

7. Many people believe that tall,
   spindly plants need
   □ a. extra water.
   □ b. more sunlight.
   □ c. more nutrients.

8. Porous containers are best
   suited for
   □ a. cactus plants.
   □ b. African violets.
   □ c. water lilies.

9. The author implies that
   □ a. ivy is the most popular
        indoor plant.
   □ b. plants can die if they are
        given too much water.
   □ c. most plants should be placed
        in a northerly window
        during winter months.

10. We can conclude that
    □ a. vegetables are easier to grow
         than flowering plants.
    □ b. plants grow indoors with
         little care.
    □ c. most plants live from three
         to five years.

The Masai are a tall, semi-nomadic people who have made their home in East Africa for the past 300 years. Over the centuries, the tribe, numbering over 100,000 people, has gone to tremendous lengths to resist cultural change.

One of the tribe's ancient beliefs is that cattle are God's reward, deserving of an exalted place in Masai society. Actually, cattle are essential to the tribe's existence, providing nourishment and shelter. The Masai are nourished by the cattle's blood and milk, which are drawn directly from live cows; the cattle's hide and dung are used to create rainproofing for Masai homesteads. As a result of this bovine reverence, the Masai have become perhaps the world's greatest cattlemen, tending a tribal herd of over 500,000 head.

Another ancient belief is that the earth brings misfortune, so Masai never hunt or forge metals. Consistent with these beliefs, few Masai plant crops or work the land. In fact, rarely do the Masai perform any salaried labors for others.

Men hold a preferred position in Masai society. Tribe elders determine the appropriate age for circumcision, at which time young tribesmen become junior warriors. As they grow older, they warriors' rank increases, along with new responsibilities and privileges, until they attain the position of retired elder.

The chief duty of the warriors is to guard the herds of cattle. These men are required to live in camps by themselves and may not marry until they reach the minimum rank of elder. Even then, the junior elder may not choose his own bride.

Masai marriages are always prearranged, with the man's family paying a dowry of cattle. Prospective brides are required to be circumcised. Once married, the young woman goes to live with her husband in his village. She is taunted and threatened by the other village women as a means of making her understand her low stature in her new home.

The new wife then takes on the responsibilities of building the homestead, which is fashioned from twigs, mud, and cattle dung. The Masai are polygamists, and wives build their houses surrounding their husbands' homes according to seniority. Although they are considered to be the property of their husbands, Masai women are given a measure of privilege. All wives have exclusive milking rights to their husbands' cows. But when their sons marry, the women, as a rite of passage, hand the cattle and their calves over to the newly married couple.

Recalling Facts

1. The Masai tribe numbers approximately
   - □ a. 100,000 people.
   - □ b. 300,000 people.
   - □ c. 500,000 people.

2. The Masai use cattle's blood and milk for
   - □ a. tribal rites.
   - □ b. paint dyes.
   - □ c. nourishment.

3. The highest rank in Masai society is
   - □ a. warrior.
   - □ b. chieftain.
   - □ c. retired elder.

4. Marital dowries are paid by
   - □ a. village residents.
   - □ b. the groom's family.
   - □ c. tribal elders.

5. Masai homesteads are built by
   - □ a. wives.
   - □ b. junior warriors.
   - □ c. elders.

Understanding the Passage

6. The author states that the Masai
   - □ a. mix well with other tribes.
   - □ b. resist cultural change.
   - □ c. are a violent people.

7. Cattle are important to the Masai because they
   - □ a. provide nourishment and shelter.
   - □ b. are used for bartering with other tribes.
   - □ c. help in working the land.

8. One ancient Masai belief is that
   - □ a. cattle are reincarnated.
   - □ b. polygamy is God's reward.
   - □ c. the earth brings misfortune.

9. Warriors are responsible for
   - □ a. guarding cattle herds.
   - □ b. hunting animals.
   - □ c. fighting other tribes.

10. The author implies Masai women
    - □ a. hold an exalted place in their society.
    - □ b. work harder than Masai men.
    - □ c. have many duties and few privileges.

24 The History of Stained Glass

All colored glass is "stained" by the integration of appropriate metal oxides or other chemical compounds in the glass manufacture. However, the term traditionally refers to an art form—the creation of stained glass windows. In the Middle Ages, this art was known simply as glazing, or the making of windows, and in France, *vitrail*.

The earliest extant stained glass windows are in the clerestory of Augusburg Cathedral in Germany, dating from the 11th century and attributed to the Tegerne monks. The technical excellence of these windows indicates that the art had originated earlier, and the Italo-Byzantine style suggests roots in a Hellenistic tradition. Another similar, significant example in LeMans Cathedral, France, also shows Byzantine influence. In England, the earliest known stained glass is in the Minster at York Abbey and is part of a 12th century panel depicting a seated king from a Jesse Tree window, which is similar to panels in the Saint Denis Cathedral in France. Some of the best examples of complete ranges of windows in the early Gothic style of the 12th and 13th centuries are in the well-known cathedrals at Canterbury and Chartres.

The 14th century is characterized by a flourishing humanism expressed by the depiction of human figures and in overall design. The discovery of silver stain or silver oxide in the early 14th century, together with the greater usage of white glass, induced the general lightening effect of windows. Nevertheless, by the 15th century, stained glass began to go into an artistic decline which persisted for two centuries.

The ability of glass painters to convey naturalistic effects was increased in the 17th century through the use of enamels which generated transparent colors when fired, thus preventing a necessity for separate regions of colored glass. Typical are the windows in New College Chapel at Oxford University painted from the cartoons, or preliminary designs, of Sir Joshua Reynolds.

In the 19th century, the revival of interest in medieval art by the pre-Raphaelites created windows which brought back some of the design and clarity of the early glass. This led to the many fine interpretations in 20th century glass seen in the New York studio designs of Louis Tiffany and Henri Matisse at Vence, France, as well as the windows at Coventry Cathedral in England. The technical rediscovery of making hand-blown glass in the late 19th century also contributed to this renaissance, because it produced a higher quality glass.

Recalling Facts

1. Glazing is another term for the
   - ☐ a. making of windows.
   - ☐ b. mixing of enamel.
   - ☐ c. application of stain.

2. The earliest stained glass windows are in the
   - ☐ a. Chartres Cathedral.
   - ☐ b. Augusburg Cathedral.
   - ☐ c. Canterbury Cathedral.

3. What centuries were characterized by the early Gothic style?
   - ☐ a. 12th and 13th
   - ☐ b. 14th and 15th
   - ☐ c. 16th and 17th

4. Silver oxide is
   - ☐ a. an enamel.
   - ☐ b. a stain.
   - ☐ c. a glaze.

5. The term *cartoons* in the context of this selection means
   - ☐ a. whitish glass.
   - ☐ b. vitrail.
   - ☐ c. sketches.

Understanding the Passage

6. What movement was responsible for the lightening effect of 14th century windows?
   - ☐ a. the use of white glass
   - ☐ b. the use of enamels
   - ☐ c. the use of hand-blown glass

7. The Louis Tiffany studios were located in
   - ☐ a. New York.
   - ☐ b. France.
   - ☐ c. Great Britain.

8. The 19th century revival in stained glass was brought about by the
   - ☐ a. Tegerne monks.
   - ☐ b. pre-Raphaelites.
   - ☐ c. French artisans.

9. Minster is another word for
   - ☐ a. a cathedral.
   - ☐ b. a type of stained glass.
   - ☐ c. metal oxides.

10. The 17th century stained glass windows were characterized by
    - ☐ a. a growing humanism.
    - ☐ b. a clarity of design.
    - ☐ c. naturalistic effects.

25 The Bay of Pigs

A key factor in the success of John Kennedy's bid for the presidency was his strong stand against the spread of communism in Cuba. He had promised that, if elected, he would try to rid the western hemisphere of communism.

Just days before Kennedy's inauguration, President Eisenhower broke off diplomatic ties with Cuba out of concern that Castro was pro-communist and, as a result, might threaten American interests. In the meantime, Kennedy had learned of a Central Intelligence Agency plan to invade Cuba and overthrow Castro. The head of the CIA assured the new president that the plan would be a success. Kennedy felt that if he didn't act, Castro would become an even greater threat. He was also worried that the Soviet Union might interpret inaction as a sign of weakness.

But Kennedy's advisors on Capitol Hill did not agree. Senator Fulbright of Arkansas warned the president that to invade Cuba would be foolish on several counts. The senator argued that the world would view an invasion as hypocritical in light of American calls against similar acts by other countries. He also felt that the chances of success were limited. Meanwhile, the public as well as America's allies were growing concerned because of rumors of a Cuban invasion. On April 12, the president pledged there would be no military conflict with Cuba involving American troops.

Three days later, American bombers disguised as Cuban aircraft and piloted by Cuban refugees launched an attack to destroy Castro's small air force. The attack failed and was presented to the world as an effort by defecting Cuban pilots to overthrow Castro. But the cover story leaked, and the world soon learned that the plot was backed by America all along.

Nonetheless, a second phase of the operation followed. Two days later, a flotilla of small boats containing 1,400 CIA-trained Cubans approached the island's southern coast, near the Bay of Pigs. As the boats neared the bay, they floundered on coral reefs, losing equipment and supplies. Also, because only a small percentage of the attackers were professional soldiers, the strike's force was rather ineffectual. Within four days, the invaders ran out of ammunition and retreated, having failed in a complete overthrow.

Not only was the mission a military fiasco, but it also represented failure on a much larger scale. The Bay of Pigs incident gave America's enemies an opportunity to point a morally accusing finger at the United States.

Recalling Facts

1. The president who served before Kennedy was
   □ a. Johnson.
   □ b. Nixon.
   □ c. Eisenhower.

2. CIA stands for
   □ a. Crisis Intervention Agency.
   □ b. Central Intelligence Agency.
   □ c. Core Intelligence Agency.

3. The Cuban air strike began on April
   □ a. 12th.
   □ b. 15th.
   □ c. 17th.

4. An advisor who discouraged the attack was
   □ a. President Eisenhower.
   □ b. Vice President Johnson.
   □ c. Senator Fulbright.

5. The Bay of Pigs naval invasion was over in
   □ a. four days.
   □ b. two days.
   □ c. four hours.

Understanding the Passage

6. Eisenhower broke off ties with Cuba because
   □ a. Cuba was pro-communist.
   □ b. Cuba had attacked the U.S.
   □ c. Castro had backed Kennedy in the election.

7. Kennedy felt that if he didn't authorize the invasion,
   □ a. he would have difficulty passing legislation.
   □ b. Cuba might attack the U.S.
   □ c. the Soviet Union would see it as a sign of weakness.

8. Kennedy was advised against the invasion because
   □ a. American military power was too weak for the mission.
   □ b. the chances of a successful mission were limited.
   □ c. it was too expensive.

9. The author states that one of the reasons the invasion failed was
   □ a. there were few professional soldiers among the attackers.
   □ b. the Cubans had more sophisticated firepower.
   □ c. there were insufficient American troops to win the battle.

10. We can infer that the Bay of Pigs incident was important because it
    □ a. signaled an end to close ties with Europe.
    □ b. represented the larger conflict with the Soviet Union.
    □ c. was the greatest disaster of the Kennedy administration.

Dowsing, also often referred to as water divination, is a method of finding things located underground, through the use of a human sensitivity which cannot be explained in scientific terms. This sensitivity seems to be present in many people, but it is not known to be associated with the five senses or the brain. Dowsing is used as an inexpensive and practical way of locating water, oil, archaeological sites, minerals, cables, drains, or pipes.

Dowsing has been practiced universally for over 2,000 years. It is thought that this ability is largely inherent in humans, but has diminished as this talent has become less needed with the advent of civilization. In recent times, it has been discouraged by scientific and religious authorities who doubt its claims.

The tools and methods of dowsing differ because it is an individualistic art. Often a dowser will know the answer through sensitivity but the answer is better transferred to him or her by some essential indication, so tools are needed. These tools are set in motion by the dowser's muscles with the movement corresponding to his or her code of signals.

Three types of dowsing tools are used today: pendulums, hands, and angle rods. Pendulums may be any size and of any material. Smaller ones are often used indoors by dowsers and applied to maps, while the larger ones are usually preferred for outdoor work. Some dowsers may use the sensitivity of their hands alone for outdoor work. Angle rods are pieces of wire bent at right angles. The handheld part usually measures eight inches and the long arm measures about eighteen inches. The rods are held freely in the hands with the long arm pointing forward. Upon approaching the hidden object, the muscles in the dowser's arms move the rods inward and down until they are in the "found" position.

Many people who possess the innate sensitivity to be good dowsers are not aware of their gift. This attitude, as do preconceived ideas, often prevents the successful use of this technique. This sensitivity must be carefully nurtured by practice and by concentrating clearly on what is sought.

The modern dowser often works in three stages: first, the dowser uses a map or plan for orientation; second, the dowser works at the location itself to confirm or correct the findings made with the map. And last, he or she carries out a test dig, looking for some form of incontrovertible evidence.

Recalling Facts

1. For how long has the art of dowsing been practiced?
   □ a. one century
   □ b. twenty centuries
   □ c. two centuries

2. What is a popular form of dowsing tool?
   □ a. human hands
   □ b. wooden rod
   □ c. metal wand

3. Human sensitivity to locating objects underground is a
   □ a. frequently used ability.
   □ b. often neglected ability.
   □ c. forgotten ability.

4. Name the object which is frequently located by experienced dowsers.
   □ a. gold
   □ b. uranium
   □ c. water

5. A modern dowser works in three
   □ a. stages.
   □ b. places.
   □ c. seasons.

Understanding the Passage

6. Dowsing tools, such as angle rods, are moved by
   □ a. the dowser's mind.
   □ b. the dowser's arm muscles.
   □ c. air currents.

7. This selection reveals that dowsing is
   □ a. not acceptable to some authorities.
   □ b. accepted by most individuals.
   □ c. widely practiced.

8. Experienced dowsers always seek
   □ a. angle rods.
   □ b. a form of incontrovertible evidence.
   □ c. an audience.

9. An appropriate title for this selection could be
   □ a. The Pseudoscience of Dowsing.
   □ b. The Science of Dowsing.
   □ c. The Individualistic Art of Dowsing.

10. Dowsing tools are often used because they
    □ a. aid in locating the object.
    □ b. add validity to the art.
    □ c. distract the audience.

From Coal to Gas

Energy-wise, the horn of plenty is running low. Because our cornucopia of fuel sources has been dwindling, the nation's vast coal reserves are cleaning up its dirty image to win a new role in the production of energy.

How can coal be converted into a cleaner-burning fuel? Essentially, common cleaning methods involve specific gravity separation inside a vessel containing a liquid. The pollutants, ash and sulfur-bearing materials, sink to the bottom of the liquid. The lighter coal material is skimmed or floated off at the top.

Meanwhile, the development of cleaner uses for coal is moving into more advanced stages. The possibility for such technology is reaching the commercial market now.

In obtaining clean forms of gaseous, liquid, and solid fuels from abundant coal reserves in the United States, these scientific techniques will help close the energy gap and lessen the danger of pollution. They will also create jobs and improve segments of the national economy.

For translation into more specific terms, a person might consider any rural area of the U.S. where there are large coal deposits and good supplies of water. Into this area might move a coal-processing complex requiring an investment of $450 million. Construction may take three or four years and provide as many as 5,000 local jobs at its peak.

As building tapers off and operations begin, the complex would provide steady employment for 1,500 to 2,000 persons. Each worker would require additional goods and services, thereby creating still more new jobs and opportunities for investment.

This is the future plan for the production of clean and inexpensive energy from domestic coal. The whole idea makes use of the fact that coal can be refined. Separate portions of it can be converted to synthetic gas, to liquid fuel, to electric power, and to solid reformed coal.

Extracting synthetic gas from coal is not exactly new. During World War II most gas being used in the U.S. was produced from coal, but it was expensive to make, distribute, and store, and it was dirty.

By contrast, present-day gasification methods produce a quality of gas with the clean characteristics of natural gas. While their economics are yet to be determined, coal-to-gas processes do remove such pollutants as sulfur and particulate matter. These are prime offenders to the environment when coal is burned directly as a fuel for electric power generation and in industrial processes.

Recalling Facts

1. During specific gravity treatment of fuels, pollutants
   - ☐ a. rise to the surface.
   - ☐ b. sink to the bottom.
   - ☐ c. dissolve.

2. One of the pollutants found in fuels is
   - ☐ a. ash.
   - ☐ b. carbon.
   - ☐ c. potassium.

3. Advanced processes for cleaning coal will be in use in the
   - ☐ a. 1990s.
   - ☐ b. year 2100.
   - ☐ c. year 2001.

4. Coal reserves in the United States are
   - ☐ a. scarce.
   - ☐ b. dwindling.
   - ☐ c. abundant.

5. A coal-processing complex might require an investment of
   - ☐ a. $10 million.
   - ☐ b. $225 million.
   - ☐ c. $450 million.

Understanding the Passage

6. For most workers, a coal-processing plant would mean
   - ☐ a. part-time employment.
   - ☐ b. seasonal employment.
   - ☐ c. year-round employment.

7. The process of extracting synthetic gas from coal was
   - ☐ a. first used during the 1940s.
   - ☐ b. developed in Europe during the 1960s.
   - ☐ c. discovered by accident during the early 1970s.

8. Traditionally, many electric power generating plants have
   - ☐ a. converted coal to steam to operate turbines.
   - ☐ b. contributed to air pollution by burning high sulfur coal.
   - ☐ c. been forced to curtail operations because of coal shortages.

9. The author feels that coal
   - ☐ a. can be used more extensively than it is being used today.
   - ☐ b. should be imported from foreign countries to reduce mining costs.
   - ☐ c. is easier to refine than any other fuel.

10. This article could have been titled
    - ☐ a. Coal Mining in the United States.
    - ☐ b. Progress in Pollution Controls.
    - ☐ c. A Crack in the Horn of Plenty.

Medical student John Hicks's mischievous temperament fostered a streak of violence in New York in the late 1700s that evolved into America's first riot. While practicing dissection of a corpse, Hicks noticed some young boys playing outside his laboratory window. As a practical joke, he extended the arm of the corpse to the boys and shouted, "This is your mother's hand! I just dug it up. Watch out or I'll smack you with it!"

The boys scattered, terrified. One youngster was particularly frightened; his mother had actually died recently. The boy ran home to relate the incident to his father, who rushed to the cemetery where he had buried his wife. To his horror, the man discovered the grave was empty.

The widower joined ranks with friends, leading them through the streets of Manhattan. The cluster expanded into a mob of hundreds, outraged at the arrogance of physicians infamous for robbing graves. The "Doctors' Mob" stormed New York Hospital, carrying bats and torches, demanding that the physicians reveal themselves.

Sensing the multitude's invective, the hospital's doctors managed to escape through rear windows. The vigilant crowd broke down the doors of the institution, ransacking laboratories and destroying every piece of equipment it found. Despite its trail of destruction, the crowd continued its mission. The multitude repeatedly explored New York's streets, hoping to locate the physician whom they believed had robbed the widower's wife's grave.

Meanwhile, Hicks had outsmarted them, seeking asylum at the residence of a prominent doctor. When he heard the crowd's approach, the medical student escaped again, taking refuge on a neighbor's roof.

Numerous prominent Americans fell victim to the mob's two-day streak of violence. John Jay, who eventually became the Chief Justice of the Supreme Court, was knocked unconscious by a rock. Alexander Hamilton begged the multitude to temper their spirits and return home. American Revolutionary hero Baron Friedrich von Steuben implored the governor to refrain from having the militia fire on the angry crowd. But after he was hit on the head with a brick, the baron changed his mind.

The governor eventually instructed his troops to fire on the mob. They killed eight rioters and injured many others. The uprising was soon over, and, ironically, the doctors could at last tend to the needs of those injured in the violence of America's first riot—an event which destroyed much and accomplished little.

*Reading Time*_____ *Comprehension Score*_____ *Words per Minute*_____

Recalling Facts

1. America's first riot took place
   in New York in the
   - [ ] a. 17th century.
   - [ ] b. 18th century.
   - [ ] c. 19th century.

2. The riot lasted for two
   - [ ] a. hours.
   - [ ] b. days.
   - [ ] c. weeks.

3. The medical student who
   taunted children with the arm
   of a corpse was John
   - [ ] a. Steuben.
   - [ ] b. Jay.
   - [ ] c. Hicks.

4. The riotous group came
   to be known as the
   - [ ] a. New York Mob.
   - [ ] b. Grave Robbers' Mob.
   - [ ] c. Doctors' Mob.

5. The first place the rioters
   attacked was
   - [ ] a. New York Hospital.
   - [ ] b. a cemetery.
   - [ ] c. a physician's home.

Understanding the Passage

6. The riot was sparked by
   - [ ] a. a fight between a doctor
     and patient.
   - [ ] b. a prank by a medical
     student.
   - [ ] c. the death of a
     prominent New Yorker.

7. We can infer that the incident
   that sparked the riot was
   - [ ] a. coincidental with the
     robbery of the
     widower's wife's grave.
   - [ ] b. an attempt to make
     children frightened of
     doctors.
   - [ ] c. an example of the
     arrogance of grave-
     robbing physicians.

8. The targets of the rioters were
   - [ ] a. grave robbers.
   - [ ] b. medical students.
   - [ ] c. physicians.

9. Alexander Hamilton was
   involved in the riot as
   - [ ] a. a mediator.
   - [ ] b. an instigator.
   - [ ] c. a rioter.

10. It is ironic that
    - [ ] a. the riot had little long-
      term effect.
    - [ ] b. the rioters received
      medical attenton from
      their enemies.
    - [ ] c. prominent Americans
      were injured by the mob.

Throwing Sticks

Throwing sticks have been utilized since the prehistoric period, and their use has continued until recently in many regions of the world. Many throwsticks, such as the knobkerrie of South African tribes, are straight wooden clubs, one to three feet in length, with a nearly circular cross-section and knobbed head. They have a simple ballistic trajectory similar to a thrown ball and a maximum range of about fifty yards. In some cultures, throwsticks of more advanced design have been created which use aerodynamic lift to aid in their flight. Typical of these throwsticks is the well-known example of the Australian boomerang.

Although it is commonly accepted that boomerangs are constructed so as to return to the thrower, most boomerangs are designed to fly with an approximately straight trajectory. A good straight-flying boomerang can be hurled about 200 yards. When compared with a simple throwstick of similar size and weight, the greater range of the boomerang is influenced by a cross-section of aerofoil shape which provides elevation as it flies through the air. This lift force does not act through the center of the aerofoil, and if the boomerang were straight, it would turn until it was broadside on the air flow. Therefore, boomerangs are curved and thrown with a spin so that the two wings rotate like the spokes of a wheel. Aboriginal Australians used these boomerangs for hunting kangaroos and as weapons in tribal conflicts.

Straight-flying and return boomerangs differ only in detail, but the latter are generally smaller and lighter. Usually, a return boomerang measures 18 to 30 inches from tip to tip, with a weight of 4 to 10 ounces, as compared with 24 to 35 inches tip to tip and a weight of 7 to 14 ounces for straight-flying types. As indicated by their name, return boomerangs can be thrown so that they return to the thrower, and in skilled hands their trajectory is often a large circle 30 yards in diameter. Unlike straight-flying boomerangs, return boomerangs must be thrown with their plane of rotation almost vertical, although near the end of the flight, the rotation is usually nearly horizontal. This "lying down" as it is often termed, is essential to a successful return flight because as the boomerang slows down and loses lift, a larger degree of the total lift has to be directed against gravity. Return boomerangs were used for bird hunting and for amusement by Australian Aborigines.

Recalling Facts

1. Most boomerangs are designed to fly in a
   - ☐ a. circle.
   - ☐ b. straight line.
   - ☐ c. curved line.

2. "Lying down" describes the motion of
   - ☐ a. a straight-flying boomerang.
   - ☐ b. a return boomerang.
   - ☐ c. either type of boomerang.

3. Return boomerangs were used for
   - ☐ a. hunting kangaroos.
   - ☐ b. amusement.
   - ☐ c. warfare.

4. What is a knobkerrie?
   - ☐ a. a throwstick
   - ☐ b. a return boomerang
   - ☐ c. a South African tribe

5. A straight-flying boomerang can be thrown
   - ☐ a. 200 yards.
   - ☐ b. 50 yards.
   - ☐ c. 30 yards.

Understanding the Passage

6. The measurements of return boomerangs from tip to tip are
   - ☐ a. 24 to 35 inches.
   - ☐ b. 18 to 30 inches.
   - ☐ c. 24 to 30 inches.

7. The measurements of straight-flying boomerangs from tip to tip are
   - ☐ a. 24 to 30 inches.
   - ☐ b. 18 to 30 inches.
   - ☐ c. 24 to 35 inches.

8. Boomerangs are curved to
   - ☐ a. provide aerodynamic lift.
   - ☐ b. facilitate ease of throwing.
   - ☐ c. encourage their return.

9. Types of boomerangs differ only in
   - ☐ a. small details.
   - ☐ b. construction materials.
   - ☐ c. method of tossing.

10. Various types of throwsticks have been in existence since the
    - ☐ a. Middle Ages.
    - ☐ b. prehistoric period.
    - ☐ c. nineteenth century.

Witchcraft is the word used to describe supposed magical powers. Generally, the word is associated with the ability to harm people or to damage their property. Since ancient times, people all over the world have believed in witches and witchcraft. Some researchers estimate that more than half the people living today still think that witches can influence their lives.

Witchcraft has a long history. According to the poet Homer, the witch Circe could turn humans into animals. The Old Testament of the Bible also includes several references to witches and witchcraft. The most famous Biblical reference to witches is the verse that exhorts, "Thou shalt not suffer a witch to live." Hundreds of years afterward, witch hunters accepted such statements as justification for the persecutions they inflicted on their accused.

Some scholars see witchcraft as a pre-Christian system of organized religion. In Europe, witchcraft can be traced back to many early religious sects. But church authorities, who felt that these beliefs threatened the Christian church, tried to stamp out alternative beliefs.

Church persecution of witches occurred in England, Germany, France, Italy, Scotland, and Spain. Joan of Arc, now France's national heroine, was burned at the stake by the English, who accused her of witchcraft. Historians estimate that between 1484 and 1782, the church condemned almost 300,000 women to death for practicing witchcraft. Many of these women suffered such horrible tortures that they confessed to witchcraft in order to avoid continued torment.

During the 1600s and 1700s, the fear of witchcraft was nearly hysterical in proportion. It spread beyond Europe into the American colonies. Churches and courts allowed gossip and rumor to be taken as evidence against the accused. There are records of children who actually testified against their own mothers. At the end of the famous Salem witch trials, nineteen innocent people had been executed for crimes they were not guilty of. The real reasons for this witch hunt can be traced back to political, financial, and religious jealousy among the townspeople. It also served as a way for the teenage girls who first began the accusations to keep receiving attention. Although the court later admitted its terrible error, nothing could erase the suffering that had been inflicted by the trials. These senseless witch hunts became an ugly blemish on the histories of both Europe and America.

Recalling Facts

1. The witch Circe could turn humans into
   - ☐ a. Homer.
   - ☐ b. witches.
   - ☐ c. animals.

2. Scholars of witchcraft see it as a
   - ☐ a. pre-Christian religious system.
   - ☐ b. reason to persecute women.
   - ☐ c. beneficial influence on everyone's life.

3. Joan of Arc was
   - ☐ a. a famous witch hunter.
   - ☐ b. burned at the stake.
   - ☐ c. England's national heroine.

4. Between 1484 and 1782, how many women did the church condemn to death?
   - ☐ a. 100,000
   - ☐ b. 300,000
   - ☐ c. 500,000

5. During the 1600s and 1700s, the fear of witchcraft
   - ☐ a. lessened considerably.
   - ☐ b. reached hysterical proportions.
   - ☐ c. vanished from Europe.

Understanding the Passage

6. Many witch hunters devoutly believed in the words of
   - ☐ a. Homer.
   - ☐ b. the Bible.
   - ☐ c. scholars of witchcraft.

7. Church persecution of witches occurred all over
   - ☐ a. Africa.
   - ☐ b. Greece.
   - ☐ c. Europe.

8. Many women confessed to being witches because they were
   - ☐ a. guilty.
   - ☐ b. frightened.
   - ☐ c. blackmailed.

9. One famous witch hunt took place in
   - ☐ a. Boston.
   - ☐ b. Salem.
   - ☐ c. Portsmouth.

10. The roots of some witch hunts can be found in
    - ☐ a. factual events.
    - ☐ b. circumstantial evidence.
    - ☐ c. gossip and rumor.

Problems of Older Americans

Older Americans represent a large consumer market. As the babyboomers age, the elderly population will be expanding even more. Yet most elderly consumers are not full participants in today's complex and affluent marketplace. Many elderly do not take advantage of the wide variety of goods and diverse methods of marketing because they prefer the older products and stores they have always known and relied upon. More often their choice of products is limited by physical impairment or fixed income restrictions.

Nutritional deficiency is a major problem of elderly Americans. One-half to one-third of the health problems of the elderly are believed to be related to nutrition. Assuming financial ability to provide nutritious meals, many elderly have inadequate diets because transportation is unavailable or they are unable to make use of it. They lack food storage facilities. They have little access to nutritional information or education. They lack motivation or the energy required to prepare meals. Those who need special diets may be unable to afford or to prepare the correct foods. Rising food prices too often erode the ability of those on fixed incomes to maintain even past standards of nutrition and food intake. The elderly who live alone are less likely to provide hot, nutritious meals for themselves.

In addition to nutritional problems, the packaging of foods discourages older Americans who buy in small quantities and cannot take advantage of unit cost savings obtained by purchasing large-size packages. Some senior citizens, particularly those who live alone, prefer smaller packages.

Many elderly consumers find their houses too large for their lifestyles or too expensive to maintain. Even minor repairs are difficult or impossible to perform, and help with the household chores is often unavailable or expensive. Many others leave their homes because of new highway construction, urban renewal projects, or because they want to retire to a warmer climate.

The choices available when the elderly contemplate a housing change include the purchase of a mobile home or a smaller house, rental of an apartment, or a room in a boarding house, rooming house, nursing home, or moving into a retirement community.

Whatever their housing needs, however, the elderly too often lack reliable information necessary to make the best decision, and they may be easily misled by enterprising salesmen or promotional advertising and make the worst possible choice. Fortunately, there are now many local, state, and government sponsored agencies designed to aid elderly citizens.

Recalling Facts

1. The number of older Americans will increase due to the
   - ☐ a. poor health care available.
   - ☐ b. present young generation.
   - ☐ c. baby boomers.

2. The limited participation of older Americans in the marketplace
   - ☐ a. is a result of income restrictions.
   - ☐ b. can be blamed on discrimination.
   - ☐ c. can be traced to indifference.

3. What fraction of all health problems are related to poor nutrition?
   - ☐ a. one-quarter
   - ☐ b. one-half
   - ☐ c. three-quarters

4. The elderly who are least likely to eat hot meals are those who
   - ☐ a. live alone.
   - ☐ b. are very active.
   - ☐ c. are overweight.

5. Elderly Americans cannot take advantage of
   - ☐ a. free medical care.
   - ☐ b. unit cost savings.
   - ☐ c. low-cost housing.

Understanding the Passage

6. The author suggests that food manufacturers could help the elderly by
   - ☐ a. printing prices in large numerals.
   - ☐ b. selling food at wholesale prices.
   - ☐ c. selling smaller quantities less expensively.

7. The author implies that
   - ☐ a. the government has few meal programs.
   - ☐ b. elderly people shop alone.
   - ☐ c. some salesmen may deceive the elderly.

8. In this article, the author explores
   - ☐ a. housing problems of the elderly.
   - ☐ b. prescription services for the elderly.
   - ☐ c. medicare programs for the elderly.

9. The author implies that elderly consumers
   - ☐ a. do not enjoy high-protein diets.
   - ☐ b. are afraid to ride on buses.
   - ☐ c. feel secure in stores they know.

10. We can conclude that elderly
    - ☐ a. residents cannot be evicted from their homes.
    - ☐ b. people spend less money than other groups in society.
    - ☐ c. consumers may pay more than others for many items.

Louis Pasteur will certainly be remembered forever as one of the nineteenth century's greatest scientists. His contributions to medicine and industry have made an enormous improvement in the lives of every human being. Pasteur's abstract discoveries solved many of the practical problems that had been plaguing both businessmen and doctors.

In his childhood, Pasteur demonstrated artistic talent, but after studying chemistry, he decided to become a scientist. As a professor of science, Louis began to examine the problem of fermentation, a type of chemical breakdown of substances by microbes, or germs. This interest in fermentation brought about a major practical improvement in France's struggling wine industry. Winemakers were losing money because they were unable to keep their wine from turning bitter. Wine exportation could not be profitable if the wine became undrinkable while sitting in storage. Pasteur realized that the microbes that entered the wine during processing were causing the wine to sour. In other words, the wine continued to ferment even after bottling. Pasteur suggested that these microbes could be killed by applying controlled heat. The use of heat as a means to kill germs became known as pasteurization.

Not only did the wine industry benefit from pasteurization, but the dairy industry found that pasteurization also preserved milk. Milk would stay fresher longer, and heat processing eliminated many of the harmful bacteria that caused illness. Currently, most of the processed milk sold in our country must be pasteurized before being sold to the customer.

Pasteur's interest in germs and bacteria also benefited the field of medicine. Pasteur demonstrated that many diseases are caused by germs multiplying in the body. Experimenting in his laboratory, Pasteur artificially weakened specific microbes and then placed these microbes in an animal's body. Discovering that the animal would develop a resistance, or immunity, to the microbe, Pasteur vaccinated sheep against a disease called anthrax and found that the sheep proceeded to develop an immunity to the disease.

Then Pasteur began to study rabies, a deadly disease spread by the bite of infected animals. One day, young Joseph Meister was bitten by a rabid dog. His parents, hearing of Pasteur's work, pleaded with him to experiment on their son. Although he was hesitant to use the vaccine on a human being, Pasteur finally agreed to vaccinate Joseph. After several anxious weeks, the vaccination treatment proved to be successful, and Joseph Meister became the first person to be cured of rabies.

Recalling Facts

1. Another word for microbes is
   - ☐ a. fermentation.
   - ☐ b. disease.
   - ☐ c. germs.

2. Pasteurization helps milk to
   - ☐ a. stay fresh for a longer period of time.
   - ☐ b. ferment into wine.
   - ☐ c. increase the amount of harmful bacteria.

3. Many diseases are caused by
   - ☐ a. experimenting with vaccines.
   - ☐ b. weakening microbes artificially.
   - ☐ c. multiplying germs in the body.

4. Pasteur vaccinated sheep against a disease called
   - ☐ a. rabies.
   - ☐ b. anthrax.
   - ☐ c. bacteria.

5. The parents of Joseph Meister
   - ☐ a. wanted Pasteur to experiment on their son.
   - ☐ b. refused to allow any experiments.
   - ☐ c. did not know Joseph had been bitten.

Understanding the Passage

6. If Pasteur had not studied chemistry, he might have become
   - ☐ a. an artist.
   - ☐ b. a winemaker.
   - ☐ c. a farmer.

7. Pasteurized wine made
   - ☐ a. the wine taste terrible.
   - ☐ b. a great financial improvement in the wine industry.
   - ☐ c. no difference to the winemakers.

8. It is probably important to drink unpasteurized milk
   - ☐ a. before meals.
   - ☐ b. very fresh.
   - ☐ c. instead of wine.

9. Before he met Joseph Meister, Pasteur had
   - ☐ a. never given any vaccines.
   - ☐ b. frequently vaccinated humans.
   - ☐ c. never vaccinated a human.

10. Today, rabies is a
    - ☐ a. curable disease.
    - ☐ b. problem in our cities.
    - ☐ c. good thing to catch.

33 Tornadoes

One of nature's most destructive forces is the tornado, a violent windstorm that takes the shape of a rotating column of air. Tornadoes almost always occur in conjunction with severe thunderstorms that produce high winds, heavy rainfall, and damaging hail. Though their cause is unknown, tornadoes are believed to be the result of the convergence of strong upward wind currents inside a storm with upper level winds above the storm.

Each year there are approximately 750 tornadoes reported throughout the United States, most of them occurring between the months of April and June. The principal reason for the springtime dominance of tornadoes is that continental United States air masses are at their highest contrast during spring months. Arctic air from Canada remains cold and dry, and tropical air from the Gulf of Mexico is warm, humid, and unstable. When contrasting air masses merge, a storm arises; the greater the air contrast, the more violent the storm will be. The United States has more tornadoes than any country in the world because this is where arctic and tropical air masses most frequently converge.

The average tornado varies in size from 500 feet to as much as 2,000 feet in diameter. "Twisters" travel at an average of 45 miles per hour, but some have been clocked at speeds upward of 60 miles per hour. Also, most tornadoes travel in a northeasterly direction. Still, it is difficult to characterize the typical tornado because they are by definition capricious and unstable.

This unpredictability makes accurate tornado forecasts difficult. Though it is possible to determine when a tornado is apt to occur, actual tornado warnings are issued only when a tornado has been sighted or reported on radar. Radar can be used to guess the storm's likely path, its speed, and the intensity of the storm. But conventional radar has limitations.

An advanced form of radar, known as Doppler, has the ability to detect the first steps in the formation of a tornado. Unlike conventional radar, Doppler tracks a thunderstorm's rotating wind system which usually precedes the development of a tornado. As a result, Doppler has provided forecasters with the ability to issue tornado warnings as much as 20 minutes prior to a storm's touchdown, compared to a warning of less than two minutes by visual sighting. Though tornadoes remain one of nature's most violent forces, the use of radar and advanced warning systems has substantially narrowed their paths of destruction.

Recalling Facts

1. Each year the U.S. has an average of
   - ☐ a. 250 tornadoes.
   - ☐ b. 500 tornadoes.
   - ☐ c. 750 tornadoes.

2. Most tornadoes occur during
   - ☐ a. spring.
   - ☐ b. summer.
   - ☐ c. fall.

3. Most tornadoes travel toward the
   - ☐ a. southeast.
   - ☐ b. northwest.
   - ☐ c. northeast.

4. The average tornado travels at a speed of
   - ☐ a. 30 mph.
   - ☐ b. 45 mph.
   - ☐ c. 60 mph.

5. Gulf of Mexico air masses are known for being
   - ☐ a. dry.
   - ☐ b. unstable.
   - ☐ c. stormy.

Understanding the Passage

6. Tornadoes almost always occur
   - ☐ a. when two similar air masses collide.
   - ☐ b. in conjunction with severe thunderstorms.
   - ☐ c. as a result of high temperatures and hail.

7. Tornadoes are difficult to forecast because they
   - ☐ a. are by definition unstable.
   - ☐ b. develop too quickly to detect on radar.
   - ☐ c. are visible only at close range.

8. The United States has more tornadoes than any other nation because of the
   - ☐ a. vast amount of flat land, which favors tornadoes.
   - ☐ b. extremes of tropical and arid climates nationwide.
   - ☐ c. frequency of converging tropical and arctic air masses.

9. Conventional radar is best used for
   - ☐ a. forecasting tornadoes.
   - ☐ b. guessing the storm's path.
   - ☐ c. gauging rainfall.

10. The author implies the advantage of Doppler radar is that it helps scientists
    - ☐ a. increase tornado warning times.
    - ☐ b. study the cause of tornadoes.
    - ☐ c. change the paths of tornadoes.

Today's Celts are the surviving descendants of an ancient race of people who once inhabited much of Great Britain. They speak a native language which has survived for over two thousand years. Variations of this Celtic language can be found in Brittany, Ireland, Wales, and Scotland. Although many people now prefer to speak English, or in Brittany, French, the Celtic language continues to be a great source of ethnic pride among its people. In fact, the official language of Ireland is Irish, not English.

The oldest available evidence about the Celts comes from Austria. Archaeological excavations have revealed several hundred early Celtic graves, which date from approximately 700 B.C. These Celts were one of the first northern European populations to make iron. Samples of Celtic metalwork have proven that they were proficient in that field. By about 500 B.C., these Austrian Celts had spread throughout France, Portugal, Spain, and the British Isles. After starting a settlement in northern Italy, they began to raid as far south as Rome. Roman historical documents record a major Celtic looting raid in 390 B.C. That same century, Celtic groups moved into the Balkan mountains, an area that is now Bulgaria and Greece. But after Rome regained its strength and conquered much of Europe, the only Celtic peoples who preserved their own culture were those in the British Isles and western France.

During the period before the Anglo-Saxons dominated Britain, the Celts were the most powerful peoples living in that region. Their society was defined by several classes. These classes included aristocrats and commoners, as well as a special educated class. The educated sector was composed of lawyers, poets, and priests. The priests, or druids, served as leaders and advisors to their people, and a form of druidic worship still exists today. The Celtic classes merged into tribes which consisted of families with a common ancestor. This tribal form of government became the forerunner of the Scottish clan system. Although a handful of tribes joined federations, the early Celts never developed into a united nation.

The earliest Celts had no organized form of writing, and the only information historians have about them comes from ancient Greek and Roman authors, as well as from archaeological remains. After Christianity began to filter into Britain, a primitive form of writing came into practice. But only during the Middle Ages did the Celts adopt the Latin alphabet.

Recalling Facts

1. The official language of
   Ireland is
   ☐ a. Irish.
   ☐ b. English.
   ☐ c. Welsh.

2. Archaeologists in Austria
   uncovered
   ☐ a. stone sculptures.
   ☐ b. graves.
   ☐ c. historical documents.

3. After Rome regained its
   strength, it
   ☐ a. capitulated to the Celts.
   ☐ b. conquered much of
       Europe.
   ☐ c. invited the Celts to a
       conference.

4. The Celtic educated class
   included
   ☐ a. aristocrats, commoners,
       and musicians.
   ☐ b. kings, soldiers, and
       diplomats.
   ☐ c. lawyers, poets, and
       priests.

5. Most information about the
   earliest Celts comes from
   ☐ a. the Scottish clan system.
   ☐ b. Irish legend.
   ☐ c. Greek and Roman
       authors.

Understanding the Passage

6. The Celts were
   ☐ a. dependent on the
       Romans for knowledge.
   ☐ b. innovative
       metalworkers.
   ☐ c. unfamiliar with iron.

7. The Celts and Romans were
   probably
   ☐ a. allies.
   ☐ b. enemies.
   ☐ c. traders.

8. Who dominated Britain after
   the Celts?
   ☐ a. the Anglo-Saxons
   ☐ b. the Romans
   ☐ c. the Balkans

9. Druids were
   ☐ a. unknown to the Celts.
   ☐ b. very important to Celtic
       tribes.
   ☐ c. a branch of Celtic
       warfare.

10. The earliest Celts probably
    passed stories on
    ☐ a. by word of mouth.
    ☐ b. in books.
    ☐ c. in scrolls.

35 The Man Behind the Braille System

The innovation of the Braille system for the blind is due to a tragic accident that took place in a harness shop outside Paris in the early 1800s. While playing with his father's leather crafting tools, three-year-old Louis Braille accidentally drove an awl into his left eye, damaging his sight. His eye became infected, the infection spread, and Braille became totally blind.

At the time, blind children commonly worked as beggars or factory laborers. Determined to avoid this dire fate for his son, Braille's father charted an educational path for him.

Louis attended school until he was 10, when he enrolled in an academy for blind children. The institution's library had only three books, all of which were engraved in oversized embossed letters so the students could learn to read. Despite the limitations of the library, Braille became a passionate reader. He also learned to play the piano, a skill he shared by instructing his fellow students in keyboard artistry.

Meanwhile, an army captain had invented a special "night writing" system of raised dots and dashes on cardboard, designed to send military messages after dark. When the system was introduced to the academy, Braille became fascinated, and sought to create an improved version.

He worked on his project secretly in bed at night. Braille soon discovered that a simple pattern of two dots across and three dots down provided numerous possibilities. He eventually created 63 combinations of raised dots representing all the letters in the French alphabet. Braille showed the new system to the institution's director, who adopted it immediately.

Braille flourished as he taught students, attended college, and served as organist at a cathedral in Paris. He discovered a way of applying his system to musical notation, and eventually began to compose. Despite his increasing successes, Braille faced hardship when the academy's director resigned. The new director disliked Braille's system, and insisted that the school return to the old system of oversized embossed letters. For years, Braille's writing system was suppressed.

Then one day, one of Braille's students happened to perform a piano recital in a fashionable Paris salon. After the applause, the student informed the audience that her talent was due to Louis Braille and his innovative system that enabled her to read and write. It is said that this disclosure changed the fate of the Braille system, which the French government adopted and introduced throughout the world.

Recalling Facts

1. Louis Braille was blinded at
   - ☐ a. birth.
   - ☐ b. age 3.
   - ☐ c. age 10.

2. The Braille writing system was invented in France in the
   - ☐ a. 18th century.
   - ☐ b. 19th century.
   - ☐ c. 20th century.

3. Braille's writing system consists of
   - ☐ a. two dots across, three dots down.
   - ☐ b. three dots across, three dots down.
   - ☐ c. three dots across, two dots down.

4. Aside from inventing a writing system for the blind, Louis Braille also invented a
   - ☐ a. typewriter for the blind.
   - ☐ b. special piano for the blind.
   - ☐ c. system for musical notation.

5. Braille's writing system fell out of favor when
   - ☐ a. the director of the academy for the blind resigned.
   - ☐ b. Braille worked as a cathedral organist.
   - ☐ c. new students had difficulty learning it.

Understanding the Passage

6. Braille's writing system was inspired by
   - ☐ a. his father.
   - ☐ b. the director of the academy for the blind.
   - ☐ c. an army captain's "night writing" system.

7. While studying at the academy for the blind, Braille also
   - ☐ a. became a talented pianist.
   - ☐ b. learned to paint.
   - ☐ c. learned harness making from his father.

8. Until the invention of the Braille writing system, blind people
   - ☐ a. could not read.
   - ☐ b. read by a military "night writing" system.
   - ☐ c. read books printed with embossed, oversized letters.

9. Braille's education was unusual for his time because
   - ☐ a. education was limited to a privileged few.
   - ☐ b. most blind children were professional beggars.
   - ☐ c. poor children were often sent to labor camps.

10. We can infer that Braille's writing system for the blind
    - ☐ a. was financially lucrative for Braille.
    - ☐ b. enhanced the lives of millions of blind people.
    - ☐ c. was difficult to master.

36 Smoking, Disease, and Death

The judgment that cigarette smoking is hazardous to health is a result of more than 40 years of research carried on by hundreds of scientists in this country and abroad. The conclusion that cigarette smoking is a significant health hazard is supported by every medical and health agency in the world which is known to have expressed an opinion on the matter.

While cigarette smokers tend to have higher death rates than non-smokers, 80 percent of the excess deaths associated with this habit are caused by three major diseases. They are lung cancer, coronary heart disease, and emphysema. Lung cancer was a rare disease before this century. Today, it is estimated that 60,000 men and women per year in the U.S. will die of this disease. Among men, it is the most common cause of death from cancer.

Cigarette smoking is the major cause of lung cancer. Although chronic irritation from certain chemical substances, radiation, viruses, occupational hazards, air pollution, and other environmental factors have been implicated in this disease, they are of small importance compared to cigarette smoking. To those who smoke, however, they can be important in increasing the risks still further. Approximately 90 percent of all primary lung cancer cases occur in people who smoke cigarettes. Laboratory studies have isolated from tobacco smoke a number of chemical compounds that can cause cancer. In addition, there are elements in smoke that interact with other compounds to promote cancer production.

Millions of tiny, rhythmically moving hairs, called cilia, protect the delicate tissues of the air tubes by propelling foreign matter, such as dust or pollen, toward the throat where it can be removed. Cigarette smoke paralyzes the cilia and inhibits the work of cells that assist in cleaning the lungs. Thus the cancer-causing and cancer-promoting compounds can accumulate on the lining of the bronchial tubes, where most cases of human lung cancer originate.

These factors explain, in part, why the risk of developing lung cancer increases with the length of time the individual has smoked, the number of cigarettes he smokes per day, the depth of his inhalation, and the level of the tar in the brand of cigarettes he uses.

The risk of developing lung cancer increases further if a smoker is exposed to certain occupational hazards. Studies show that asbestos workers who smoke have a risk 92 times higher than nonsmokers of the same age.

Recalling Facts

1. Research on cigarette smoking
   has been conducted over a
   period of
   ☐ a. 20 years.
   ☐ b. 30 years.
   ☐ c. 40 years.

2. Every year in the U.S., lung
   cancer takes the lives of
   ☐ a. 60,000 people.
   ☐ b. 110,000 people.
   ☐ c. 170,000 people.

3. When a person smokes, the
   cilia of his air tubes are
   ☐ a. destroyed.
   ☐ b. strengthened.
   ☐ c. paralyzed.

4. Most lung cancer originates
   in the
   ☐ a. lungs.
   ☐ b. bronchial tubes.
   ☐ c. trachea.

5. A substance in cigarettes
   mentioned is
   ☐ a. tar.
   ☐ b. nicotine.
   ☐ c. formaldehyde.

Understanding the Passage

6. Lung cancer was a rare disease in
   the 1800s because
   ☐ a. air pollution was not a
       problem.
   ☐ b. people did not smoke
       as much.
   ☐ c. cigarettes did not contain
       harmful substances.

7. Studies show that asbestos fiber
   ☐ a. cleans the cilia of the
       breathing passages.
   ☐ b. causes pneumonia in
       factory workers.
   ☐ c. contributes to the
       development of lung cancer.

8. Heavy smoking can cause
   ☐ a. heart difficulties.
   ☐ b. an ulcer.
   ☐ c. a stroke.

9. The author implies that
   ☐ a. some viruses are caused by
       smoking.
   ☐ b. the desire to smoke is
       inherited.
   ☐ c. nonsmokers sometimes
       develop lung cancer.

10. The reader can conclude that
    ☐ a. smoking is harmful to health.
    ☐ b. smoking is a controversial
        subject.
    ☐ c. some experts will not admit
        that smoking is dangerous.

37 Remember the Alamo!

In the early 1800s, Mexico asked some Americans to found colonies in Texas, its territory north of the Rio Grande River. This invitation set the stage for a conflict that would give rise to one of the world's most famous battle cries.

The Mexicans had wanted Americans to help populate lands controlled by enemy Indians. In return, the new settlers were given free land and Mexican citizenship. The problem was that the new citizens objected to the lack of freedom under Mexican rule. In an effort to control these free thinkers, Mexican General Santa Ana marched his troops into Texas, declared himself dictator, and moved to attack a garrison known as the Alamo.

The commander of the Texas troops was Colonel William Travis, a 27-year-old lawyer. He led 145 men in the defense of the Alamo, including the legendary heroes Davy Crockett and Jim Bowie. But the troops' belief in their fight for freedom proved to be no match for the sheer numbers of Mexican soldiers—six to seven thousand by some counts.

The battle began on February 23, 1836. Within three weeks, Santa Ana's troops stormed the Alamo, killing every Texan soldier to the man. The only survivors of the battle were a lieutenant's widow and a servant. Santa Ana took the survivors prisoner and sent them to Texas General Sam Houston. The Mexican leader offered Houston peace and amnesty if he would lay down his arms and submit to Mexican rule.

Outraged by Santa Ana's offer so soon after the bloody massacre at the Alamo, Houston rallied his troops to retaliate against the Mexican general. On April 21, Houston led 600 Texans to Santa Ana's riverside encampment at San Jacinto. He implored his men to remember their fallen comrades and urged them to fight for the cause of independence.

With a shout of "Remember the Alamo!" the Texans rushed to the attack, defeating the Mexican army. The troops killed 700 Mexicans and took over 600 prisoners, including General Santa Ana. In so doing, Houston's men won freedom for Texas. Nine years later, Texas was annexed to the United States.

Some historians cite the Texans' battle for independence as an early example of American aggression, because the territory legally belonged to Mexico. But most Texans view the conflict as a revolt against Mexican injustice, and to this day, carry the battle of the Alamo close to their hearts.

Recalling Facts

1. The commander of the Texas troops at the Alamo was
   - ☐ a. Davy Crockett.
   - ☐ b. William Travis.
   - ☐ c. Sam Houston.

2. Mexican troops who stormed the Alamo numbered about
   - ☐ a. 6,000.
   - ☐ b. 600.
   - ☐ c. 145.

3. The battle of the Alamo took place in
   - ☐ a. 1836.
   - ☐ b. 1845.
   - ☐ c. 1863.

4. In return for settling in Texas, Americans were given
   - ☐ a. livestock and homesteads.
   - ☐ b. the Alamo.
   - ☐ c. Mexican citizenship.

5. The cry "Remember the Alamo!" was first used at the
   - ☐ a. battle of the Alamo.
   - ☐ b. battle at San Jacinto.
   - ☐ c. annexation of Texas.

Understanding the Passage

6. The Mexican government asked Americans to settle in Texas to help populate areas controlled by
   - ☐ a. Spanish settlers.
   - ☐ b. rebellious Mexicans.
   - ☐ c. enemy Indians.

7. Texas settlers fought for independence from Mexico because they
   - ☐ a. wanted to rule over Mexico.
   - ☐ b. objected to their lack of freedom.
   - ☐ c. hoped to be annexed by the United States.

8. The purpose of the battle at San Jacinto was to
   - ☐ a. retaliate for the massacre at the Alamo.
   - ☐ b. free Texas prisoners of war.
   - ☐ c. recapture land from Santa Ana.

9. The cry "Remember the Alamo!" is a reminder to remember
   - ☐ a. the fallen Texas troops at the Alamo.
   - ☐ b. Santa Ana's declaration of dictatorship.
   - ☐ c. the fight for land controlled by Indians.

10. The author states that some historians view Texans' fight for independence as
    - ☐ a. a futile effort.
    - ☐ b. an example of American aggression.
    - ☐ c. a cowardly revolt.

38 Health for Deprived Children

Poor children who are especially vulnerable to health problems, are in special need of good health care, but most of them do not have it. Their families seek out medical care for serious illnesses or injuries, but poor children are much less likely to get continuing preventive care. In our urban and rural slums, neglected health problems are common facts of life. Serious illnesses and handicaps often develop needlessly. In low-income areas served by the Children and Youth Projects, these conditions are being countered by good health care that is readily available and acceptable to the families. So far, about half a million children and teenagers in low-income areas across the country have been enrolled in C & Y projects.

Each child enrolled is in a plan of continuous health supervision that deals with the whole range of his medical, dental, and emotional health needs. He is periodically examined and tested for health problems and receives preventive care, diagnostic services, treatment, correction of defects, and aftercare. He is served not only by doctors, nurses, and dentists, but also by nutritionists, social workers, psychologists, speech and hearing specialists, physical and occupational therapists, and many other types of personnel who get to know the child and his family over a period of time, and so are able to give personalized attention. Besides giving care, the staff counsels families about what they can do to protect their children's health and how to make good use of health services. While the health services are for children, the C & Y projects are family-centered, since the solutions to many child health problems are to be found through working with the parents. The projects put heavy emphasis on reaching out to the families to provide services, rather than giving service only as requested.

In working to meet the total health needs of the children, the C & Y projects rely to a great extent on other health, education, and social agencies in the communities. Cooperating with these agencies and making maximum use of their services are important features of the program.

Healthier children are the most important result of C & Y projects. There are others: families who know more about how to care for their health; low-income communities that have a voice in how their health care needs will be met, and institutions, agencies, and health workers who have a better idea of what is involved in promoting the health of poor children.

Recalling Facts

1. How many children and
   teenagers are enrolled in
   C & Y projects?
   □ a. half a million
   □ b. one million
   □ c. two million

2. C & Y projects are
   □ a. independently operated.
   □ b. interrelated.
   □ c. government sponsored.

3. The C & Y project emphasizes
   □ a. continuous service.
   □ b. disease diagnosis.
   □ c. emergency treatment.

4. In this article, the author
   mentions
   □ a. hearing specialists.
   □ b. optometrists.
   □ c. research consultants.

5. C & Y health care is
   □ a. readily available.
   □ b. widely advertised.
   □ c. generally ignored.

Understanding the Passage

6. The author states that poor
   families generally
   □ a. receive free hospital care.
   □ b. do not respond to their
       children's needs.
   □ c. seek medical attention only
       in emergencies.

7. One of the functions of C & Y
   projects is to
   □ a. instruct parents in child
       health care.
   □ b. tutor children in school
       subjects.
   □ c. plan educational trips
       around the country.

8. C & Y projects help mothers to
   □ a. plan well-balanced meals.
   □ b. balance their budgets.
   □ c. shop for inexpensive
       clothing.

9. The author implies that
   □ a. C & Y projects help to
       rehabilitate drug addicts.
   □ b. elderly people are served by
       C & Y projects.
   □ c. handicaps are often the
       result of neglected illnesses.

10. We can conclude that personnel
    in the C & Y project
    □ a. become well aquainted with
        the families they serve.
    □ b. were once poor people
        themselves.
    □ c. live in the homes of the
        deprived children they serve.

39 Income Tax

The United States income tax has played an important role in American history for over a century. It was first used in this country as a means of financing the Civil War. Many casualities and dollars later, the war ended, and the need for an income tax dwindled.

During the 1890s, a new battle arose: a fiscal depression. Efforts were made to establish a regular income tax, but these attempts were thwarted by a Supreme Court decision in 1895. The court declared that an income tax would breach the constitutional provision requiring taxes to be apportioned among the states according to population.

Corporate America was first called upon in 1909 to help foot the bill of running the government. At that time, Congress enacted a corporate income tax bill, designed to be a kind of fee for the privilege of doing business.

Congress soon realized that American businesses alone could not answer the financial needs of a growing government—the people, too, would have to be taxed. So, in 1913 the 16th Amendment to the Constitution was adopted, eliminating the state apportionment requirement. The first income tax mandated a maximum rate of six percent on incomes greater than $500,000.

The six percent rate escalated rapidly with the onset of World War I, much to the consternation of wealthy Americans. Amid cries of "socialist finance," the tax was eventually relaxed. By the 1920s, the Treasury Department coffers were overflowing with a budget surplus. The decade, however, ended with a financial bang as the stock market collapsed in 1929. The crash required some stiffening of rates, but the income tax still effected a relatively small percentage of the population. At the onset of World War II, only four to five million Americans were required to pay a personal income tax.

However, the cost of financing the war created new strains on the federal budget. The income tax had to be changed to include more Americans. Exemptions were decreased, rates were raised and a broader base of Americans were taxed. A withholding tax was introduced, meaning taxes would be collected directly from workers' paychecks.

World War II proved to be a crossroads for the income tax. Since that time, many changes have been instituted, with tax laws that now come and go on an annual basis. But despite the ebb and flow of regulations, one thing remains certain—taxes will be with us for a long time to come.

Recalling Facts

1. An income tax was first used as a means of financing
   - a. the American Revolution.
   - b. the Civil War.
   - c. World War I.

2. A corporate income tax was first instituted in
   - a. 1895.
   - b. 1909.
   - c. 1913.

3. The 16th Amendment to the Constitution provides for
   - a. two houses of Congress.
   - b. a Supreme Court.
   - c. an income tax.

4. The first income tax mandated a maximum rate of
   - a. six percent.
   - b. eight percent.
   - c. twelve percent.

5. At the onset of World War II, the number of Americans required to pay an income tax was
   - a. one to two million.
   - b. four to five million.
   - c. eight to nine million.

Understanding the Passage

6. The significance of the Supreme Court decision of 1895 is that it
   - a. spurred the movement to establish a regular income tax.
   - b. required corporate America to pay taxes.
   - c. declared the income tax unconstitutional.

7. One effect of the stock market crash of 1929 was to
   - a. increase tax rates.
   - b. eliminate corporate taxes.
   - c. broaden the tax base.

8. The purpose of the withholding tax is to
   - a. collect taxes directly from workers' paychecks.
   - b. provide an automatic exemption for employees.
   - c. prevent taxes from increasing.

9. World War II proved to be a crossroads for the income tax because
   - a. it was the first time taxes were used to finance a war.
   - b. the expense of the war required changes in the tax system.
   - c. the war created a budget surplus.

10. The author implies that the system of taxing the public
    - a. becomes simpler each year.
    - b. is highly efficient.
    - c. changes annually.

Because cell energy and essential cellular building blocks are derived from food, some cancer researchers have turned to a study of nutrition. The main sources of energy are carbohydrates and fats. Proteins are necessary not only as energy sources, but as cell building blocks. In addition to these major diet components, the body requires minerals, salts, and vitamins. There is no diet known to prevent cancer in man. And treatment of cancer by diet alone is not accepted by most doctors.

In general, both normal and cancer cells have the same nutrient requirements. However, one amino acid, asparagine, is manufactured in large quantities in normal cells but is not synthesized or produced by some cancer cells. Thus, such cells must obtain asparagine from the body's extracellular fluids. The enzyme that can break down asparagine has been used to inhibit some tumors in animals by destroying the asparagine in their food supply. It is also useful in certain patients with acute leukemia, whose leukemic cells require asparagine for growth. However, there are more direct ways in which nutrition affects the development of cancers. A Chicago investigator showed that by cutting the food intake of mice by one-third, at which level the animals were quite healthy, but not so fat, the occurrence of breast cancers was reduced by 50 percent. Such changes in diet as those that produce severe weight loss in laboratory animals also affect tumor growth. However, cancers continue to grow under a variety of dietary conditions, including starvation.

At the time these laboratory experiments were being performed, a study of insurance policy holders also indicated a higher occurrence of cancers among those who were overweight at the time of their insurance examination than among those of normal or below-average weight. However, more recent studies seem to indicate that there is no general increase in cancer related to excess weight in man.

The development and growth of certain specific cancers in animals can be modified by vitamins, minerals, and salts. For instance, several investigators have reported a protective effect against cancers of the bronchus and uterus in experimental animals when vitamin A was administered. There is some evidence that vitamin deficiency in man plays a role in the occurrence of cancers of the oral cavity and the esophagus. If such deficiency exists, it is probably only one of a number of factors to be considered.

Recalling Facts

1. Body cells are strengthened by
   ☐ a. carbohydrates.
   ☐ b. fats.
   ☐ c. proteins.

2. Asparagine is described as
   ☐ a. an anti-cancer drug.
   ☐ b. an amino acid.
   ☐ c. a natural hormone.

3. Leukemic cells require asparagine for
   ☐ a. growth.
   ☐ b. division.
   ☐ c. resiliency.

4. A Chicago investigator experimented with cancer in
   ☐ a. rabbits.
   ☐ b. guinea pigs.
   ☐ c. mice.

5. The bronchus and uterus can be protected against cancer with
   ☐ a. iodized salt.
   ☐ b. vitamin A.
   ☐ c. potassium.

Understanding the Passage

6. According to the author, some cancer cells are
   ☐ a. much larger than normal cells.
   ☐ b. unable to manufacture asparagine.
   ☐ c. usually killed with vitamins.

7. Latest cancer research shows that
   ☐ a. humans can contract cancer from animals.
   ☐ b. reducing food intake decreases the possibility of cancer.
   ☐ c. mouth cancer may be caused by vitamin deficiencies.

8. A study of insurance policy holders who developed cancer showed that
   ☐ a. cancer and excessive weight are related.
   ☐ b. cancer victims buy the most expensive policies.
   ☐ c. no relationship exists between cancer and virus infections.

9. The author has no faith in
   ☐ a. doctors who treat cancer with radiation.
   ☐ b. diets that allegedly prevent cancer.
   ☐ c. researchers who subject animals to dangerous drugs.

10. The article suggests that cancer cells
    ☐ a. are really dead cells.
    ☐ b. feed on neighboring cells.
    ☐ c. survive under the same conditions as normal cells.

Wolfgang Amadeus Mozart was one of the few child prodigies who made a lasting and significant impact on the world of classical music. Born in Austria in 1756, Mozart was most greatly influenced by his father, Leopold, a talented violinist. Leopold took his gifted child to various courts and castles throughout Europe to display his amazing musical talents. By the age of six, Mozart had performed for Austrian royalty.

Mozart's gift as a performer was matched by his ability to compose. By the time he was eight, he had written a symphony and numerous piano pieces. Thanks to his travels throughout Europe, the young composer was exposed to a variety of musical styles—Italian opera, French orchestral pieces, and German religious works. These early influences appeared in his work throughout his life.

As he grew older, Mozart found it increasingly difficult to earn a living. He was appointed the Konzertmeister to the archbishop of Salzburg, a position rich in prestige and creative freedom, but poor in financial reward. A few years after the appointment, the archbishop died, leaving Mozart bereft of a sympathetic patron.

Mozart then moved to Vienna where he tried with little reward to make a living as a composer and performer. Despite his hardships, he wrote rapidly. He composed his Symphony No. 36, the "Linz," rehearsed it, and had it performed within a period of four days. The overture to "Don Giovanni," perhaps his most famous opera, was composed in its entirety the night before its debut.

Throughout his life, Mozart's work was financially unappreciated. Only in the last year of his life, at the age of 35, did he begin to get commissions for his music. As the new-found interest in his artistry began, however, Mozart's physical strength declined.

He developed typhus, a deadly condition exacerbated by his grueling composing schedule. While Mozart battled the disease, a rumor spread that he had been poisoned by a popular composer, Salieri, who was both Mozart's friend and rival. An autopsy was never performed, but it is almost certain that Salieri was not responsible for Mozart's death.

Mozart was given a pauper's funeral in Vienna. Few friends were present, and he was buried in an unmarked grave. Despite his tragic end, Mozart left behind a rich musical tradition, providing a living tribute to his genius. His music today comprises a portrait of the classical style in its most masterful expression.

Recalling Facts

1. One of Mozart's earliest influences was
   - ☐ a. Leopold Mozart.
   - ☐ b. the archbishop of Salzburg.
   - ☐ c. Don Giovanni.

2. Mozart wrote his first symphony at the age of
   - ☐ a. six.
   - ☐ b. eight.
   - ☐ c. twelve.

3. When Mozart lived in Vienna, he worked as a
   - ☐ a. carpenter.
   - ☐ b. Konzertmeister.
   - ☐ c. composer.

4. Mozart's Symphony No. 36 is also known as
   - ☐ a. "Leopold."
   - ☐ b. "Linz."
   - ☐ c. "Don Giovanni."

5. Salieri was Mozart's
   - ☐ a. father.
   - ☐ b. cousin.
   - ☐ c. friend.

Understanding the Passage

6. We can infer that Mozart's
   - ☐ a. accomplishments were lasting.
   - ☐ b. early travels spoiled his education.
   - ☐ c. abilities were overrated.

7. One of Mozart's greatest difficulties was
   - ☐ a. composing orchestral pieces.
   - ☐ b. performing before royalty.
   - ☐ c. earning a living.

8. An important musical influence was
   - ☐ a. European folk music.
   - ☐ b. Italian opera.
   - ☐ c. Eastern religion.

9. The author implies that Mozart's music
   - ☐ a. was widely popular during his lifetime.
   - ☐ b. gained popularity at the end of his life.
   - ☐ c. was never popular.

10. Mozart probably died from
    - ☐ a. typhus.
    - ☐ b. poisoning.
    - ☐ c. old age.

42

The Quiet Charm of Sandwich

Heritage Plantation, sprawling on the hill above the town of Sandwich, Cape Cod, Massachusetts, offers a Shaker round barn, which shelters an impressive collection of antique cars, a military museum, a windmill, and a rhododendron garden.

The round, stone barn is modeled after one built in 1826 by the Shakers of Hancock, Massachusetts, who felt the design provided more efficient workspace than the conventional barn. The correctness of their theory may be debatable, but there can be no argument that the arrangement is most suitable for displaying the collection of automobiles. Thirty-five cars in mint condition can be shown on the circular balcony and lower floor. The oldest vehicle on view is an 1899 Winton, a true horseless carriage.

The Military Museum building is a replica of the Publick Building constructed for the Continental Army at New Windsor, New York, in 1783. In the building is a display of antique firearms representing a cross-section of weaponry, but with emphasis on guns important in American history. Also in the museum is a collection of nearly 2,000 hand-painted, finely detailed miniature soldiers. The figures depict the American soldier in uniform and colors of his regiment from 1621 to 1900.

Rambling through the 76 acres that make up the Plantation are rustic but well-kept trails that lead past hundreds of exotic plantings of rhododendron and mountain laurel. A textile manufacturer and horticulturist named Dexter acquired the property in 1921, and devoted the next 23 years to crossing local stock with plants from around the world. The beauty of the resulting Dexter Hybrids defies description when they are in bloom in the late spring and early summer. The rhododendrons are interspersed among the native pines, oaks, maples, hollies, and beeches that have been supplemented with many other trees.

The basic charm of Sandwich can be appreciated year-round. There is the quiet New England dignity of the town that is somehow preserved even at the height of the vacation madness. There is the serenity of an old cemetery, whose Revolutionary War veterans lie under somber slate gravestones. There are the Cape Cod houses whose weathered, silver-gray cedar shingles and bright trim are as appropriate to the setting as the lobster pots stacked casually beside the houses. And there are the roads that lead to the salt marshes, to the spectacular white dunes of Sandy Neck, and the sea. Visiting the town of Sandwich is like taking a step back in time.

*Reading Time*_____ *Comprehension Score*_____ *Words per Minute*_____

Recalling Facts

1. At the Heritage Plantation, a visitor can find a
   - ☐ a. gristmill.
   - ☐ b. sawmill.
   - ☐ c. windmill.

2. The oldest antique car in the museum is a
   - ☐ a. Cord.
   - ☐ b. Stanley Steamer.
   - ☐ c. Winton.

3. The Military Museum is a replica of a building located in
   - ☐ a. Connecticut.
   - ☐ b. New York.
   - ☐ c. Pennsylvania.

4. The Military Museum contains a collection of miniature
   - ☐ a. weapons.
   - ☐ b. soldiers.
   - ☐ c. fortresses.

5. How many years did Dexter devote to creating his hybrids?
   - ☐ a. nearly 10 years
   - ☐ b. more than 20 years
   - ☐ c. almost 40 years

Understanding the Passage

6. The Shaker barn was built in a round shape because it
   - ☐ a. blended with the environment.
   - ☐ b. was a common design at the time.
   - ☐ c. provided better workspace.

7. We can assume that
   - ☐ a. soldiers were present in America in the early 1620s.
   - ☐ b. guns were not used in war until after 1800.
   - ☐ c. Civil War uniforms were manufactured in New Jersey.

8. Information in the article suggests that early tombstones were
   - ☐ a. large and ornate.
   - ☐ b. made of slate.
   - ☐ c. often stolen.

9. We can assume that
   - ☐ a. the population of Sandwich drops drastically in winter.
   - ☐ b. Sandwich is really a small island.
   - ☐ c. people visit Sandwich year-round.

10. At the Heritage Plantation, a visitor may
    - ☐ a. hunt.
    - ☐ b. walk.
    - ☐ c. swim.

43

The First Woman Cabinet Member

Frances Perkins was a noted public servant and labor reformer who won her greatest fame as the first female cabinet member in American history. Perkins served as Labor Secretary during the presidency of Franklin Roosevelt.

Born in Boston in 1880, Perkins faced many challenges in her early years. She attended a primarily male high school, and then went on to Mount Holyoke College, where she earned a bachelor's degree in chemistry and physics.

After college, Perkins became a high school science teacher. During her spare time, she worked in welfare centers in Chicago, collecting wages for workers who had been cheated by their bosses. This experience was her first exposure to labor unions. It provided her with a basic understanding of and empathy for the American worker and gave her an urge to learn more.

Perkins moved to New York City and attended Columbia University, where she earned a master's degree in economics and sociology. She then set out on her life's career of championing the causes of working people.

Perkins became the executive secretary of the New York Consumers' League and of the city's Committee on Safety. She became an ardent supporter of the need for safe work environments, a cause made more passionate by a factory fire she witnessed in which over 100 workers died.

Over the next 15 years, Perkins became a prominent figure in New York politics. She served on the state's Industrial Commission, a job that made Perkins the first woman to occupy the position, as well as the highest paid state employee in the United States. She also became an expert on unemployment insurance and a strong ally of the governor—Franklin D. Roosevelt.

When Roosevelt was elected president, he named Perkins Secretary of Labor because he felt she would be sensitive to workers' problems during the Depression. Perkins served in the cabinet until shortly after Roosevelt's death in 1945. During her years of service, she played an important role in shaping the Social Security Act and the Fair Labor Standards Act. She also became a strong figure in resolving disputes between labor and management. Through it all she earned the hard-won respect of labor leaders.

Perkins's many contributions made an indelible imprint on the face of labor. Not only was she the first woman cabinet member, she was also one of the nation's most dedicated and successful public servants.

Recalling Facts

1. During the Roosevelt presidency, Frances Perkins served as
   - ☐ a. Secretary of the Industrial Commission.
   - ☐ b. Executive of the Consumers' League.
   - ☐ c. Secretary of the Department of Labor.

2. Frances Perkins was born in
   - ☐ a. Boston.
   - ☐ b. Chicago.
   - ☐ c. New York City.

3. Aside from being the first woman cabinet member, Perkins was also the first woman to
   - ☐ a. head the New York Consumers' League.
   - ☐ b. serve on New York's Industrial Commission.
   - ☐ c. earn a master's degree from Columbia University.

4. While at Columbia, Perkins earned a master's degree in
   - ☐ a. chemistry and physics.
   - ☐ b. labor relations.
   - ☐ c. economics and sociology.

5. Perkins first came to know Roosevelt when he was
   - ☐ a. mayor of New York City.
   - ☐ b. governor of New York.
   - ☐ c. President of the United States.

Understanding the Passage

6. Perkins first became interested in labor issues when she
   - ☐ a. worked in Chicago's welfare centers.
   - ☐ b. was a graduate student at Columbia.
   - ☐ c. served as Labor Secretary.

7. Perkins strongly supported on-the-job safety issues after she
   - ☐ a. had been injured while teaching high school.
   - ☐ b. had witnessed a factory fire that killed some workers.
   - ☐ c. lost her parents in labor-related accidents.

8. We can infer that Perkins
   - ☐ a. held radical political beliefs.
   - ☐ b. was dedicated to various labor causes.
   - ☐ c. was a feminist.

9. Roosevelt named Perkins to a cabinet post because he
   - ☐ a. felt she would be sensitive to Depression-era workers.
   - ☐ b. wanted a female cabinet member.
   - ☐ c. remembered her loyalty during his governorship.

10. The author implies that Perkins's work for labor issues was
    - ☐ a. considered unfeminine behavior.
    - ☐ b. resented by labor union leaders.
    - ☐ c. highly effective.

Alfred Nobel was a shy, quiet Swedish bachelor who set the world on fire with an important discovery. He invented dynamite.

Nobel became rich as a result of his invention, but had difficulty enjoying his newfound wealth. He was consumed with guilt for having created such a deadly explosive. He chose to use his money to reward people who "contributed most materially to the benefit of mankind." In 1895, while visiting the Swedish Club of Paris, Nobel drew up a handmade will signing over his fortune to establish the Nobel Prizes. Within two weeks he was dead.

Despite the rather unofficial nature of the handmade will, the Nobel Foundation was formed with the purpose of seeing that Nobel's dream was realized. The foundation is run by six board members whose job it is to oversee the investment of Nobel's original $9 million. That sum has since grown to $37 million thanks to investments in Swedish real estate, the American stock market, and other types of securities.

In the beginning, the foundation established five awards—literature, physics, chemistry, medicine, and peace. The prize for literature is voted by the Swedish Academy, which is made up of 18 writers. The prizes for physics and chemistry are chosen by the Swedish Academy of Science. Sweden's leading hospital, the Caroline Institute, is responsible for choosing the winner of the prize for medicine. It is voted by the hospital's staff of 45 physicians.

The peace prize award is decided somewhat differently. Nobel had a lifelong desire to draw his native Sweden closer to Norway, and as a result, he instructed the peace prize be voted by a Norwegian group. Each year five prominent Norwegians, appointed by their government, determine who wins the peace prize, perhaps the most revered award in the world.

These five prizes were the only ones given until 1968, when a prize for excellence in economics was added to the Nobel list. In addition to their responsibility for the physics and chemistry prizes, the Swedish Academy of Sciences selects the recipient of the economics prize.

The awards are handed out each year on December 10, the anniversary of Nobel's death. The ceremonies take place in both Oslo and Stockholm, where every winner receives a gold medal, a certificate, and cash ranging in amounts from $30,000 to $125,000. The Nobel Prize is the ultimate certificate of work toward a most admirable purpose—"the benefit of mankind."

Recalling Facts

1. Nobel established the Nobel Prizes in the
   - ☐ a. 18th century.
   - ☐ b. 19th century.
   - ☐ c. 20th century.

2. In the beginning, the Nobel foundation established
   - ☐ a. seven awards.
   - ☐ b. six awards.
   - ☐ c. five awards.

3. Nobel was born in
   - ☐ a. Sweden.
   - ☐ b. Norway.
   - ☐ c. Paris.

4. The prize for medicine is voted by the
   - ☐ a. Swedish Academy.
   - ☐ b. Swedish Academy of Science.
   - ☐ c. Caroline Institute.

5. The prizes are awarded on the anniversary of
   - ☐ a. the founding of Norway.
   - ☐ b. Nobel's death.
   - ☐ c. Nobel's birth.

Understanding the Passage

6. The author implies Nobel is most famous for
   - ☐ a. his wealth.
   - ☐ b. inventing dynamite.
   - ☐ c. founding the Nobel prizes.

7. Nobel established the prizes because he
   - ☐ a. felt guilty about having invented dynamite.
   - ☐ b. had no family to whom he could leave his money.
   - ☐ c. wanted to be remembered in history.

8. The author implies that the most respected award is the
   - ☐ a. medicine prize.
   - ☐ b. peace prize.
   - ☐ c. literature prize.

9. The peace prize is voted by prominent Norwegians because
   - ☐ a. Norway is the most peace-loving nation.
   - ☐ b. Nobel wanted Norway to be closer to Sweden.
   - ☐ c. Nobel was born in Norway.

10. Nobel's purpose for establishing the prizes was to reward people who most contributed to the
    - ☐ a. world's wealth.
    - ☐ b. advancement of science.
    - ☐ c. benefit of mankind.

45   Basketry: A Stone Age Craft

Basket making is a very ancient craft. Fragments of basketwork have been excavated from European Stone Age dwellings dated at about 9000 B.C. Early humans not only used basketry to make storage containers, but also as a building material, a framework for boats, for shields and armor, and for fish traps.

The materials employed for constructing baskets come from plants whose flexibility and durability allow them to be woven. In Europe, the customary materials for basket making are one- and two-year-old growths of hazel and willow and for "softer" basketry, straw is used. In Asia, the most commonly used materials are raffia, which is the shredded leaves of a tropical palm, and rattan, or cane, which is the long stems of a Southeast Asian palm. Timber may also be split and cut lengthwise to provide long, flat widths of basketry material. In Europe, the willow and hazel are used in this manner. Additionally, these materials and cane need to be soaked in water before use, to make them sufficiently malleable for weaving.

There are two major types of basketwork: that which is made by coiling and that which is woven. The softer natural materials are used for coiled baskets, while the stiffer natural materials are used for woven baskets.

Coiled basketry is rendered from long strips of fibrous materials which may be in the form of rods, but are commonly plaits, ropes, or simple bundles. The strip is coiled upon itself and fastened by stitching, or wrapping a separate strip around the coil. There are many different methods in which wrapping may be accomplished, the names of which are attributed to New World peoples, such as the Navajo of the Southwest, who are proficient in this kind of basketry. In Europe, coiled straw basketry was often used to construct beehives and floor mats.

Woven baskets may have a wooden base onto which are placed the upright rods to be woven, but usually two groups of rods are set at right angles and their centers intertwined to form the slath, or starting point. The rods are separated like the spokes of a wheel and further rods are spirally woven in and out around this slath. Once this base is adequately large and workable, the radial rods are bent upwards to form the sides of the basket, and weaving continues until the basket reaches the desired height.

Recalling Facts

1. A slath is a
   □ a. tree-climbing animal.
   □ b. starting point in a basket.
   □ c. form of basketry.

2. What are two types of basket making?
   □ a. coiled and woven
   □ b. rod and spiral
   □ c. raffia and cane

3. The traditional fibrous substance used in European basketry is
   □ a. ten-year growth of raffia.
   □ b. one- and two-year growths of willow.
   □ c. one-year growth of banana leaves.

4. In additon to grasses, some woven baskets contain
   □ a. a wooden base.
   □ b. a cloth lining.
   □ c. earth pigments.

5. The wrapping of coiled basketwork is named according to the
   □ a. type of material.
   □ b. native American group.
   □ c. form of rods.

Understanding the Passage

6. This selection hints that basketry materials
   □ a. may last for centuries.
   □ b. are of a delicate nature.
   □ c. can be used to date abandoned villages.

7. A non-European basketry material is
   □ a. rattan.
   □ b. willow.
   □ c. hazel.

8. Rods are usually the framework of
   □ a. coiled basketwork.
   □ b. woven basketwork.
   □ c. coiled and woven basketwork.

9. In Europe, coiled straw basketry was once used to construct
   □ a. fish traps.
   □ b. frameworks for boats.
   □ c. beehives.

10. What form of basketry are softer fibrous materials used for?
   □ a. coiled
   □ b. woven
   □ c. both coiled and woven

Yorktown was established in 1691. During the early 1700s, the town grew and prospered because of the rich tobacco trade that passed through its harbor and warehouses. Its prosperity reached a peak around 1750, when there was a population of about 2,500, including a number of wealthy merchant families with fine homes. With the gradual decline of the Virginia tobacco trade, the importance of the town dwindled.

Yorktown, though smaller than in colonial days, continues as an active community. Several of the houses and other structures of colonial times are still standing and give the town much of the character of a long-vanished period. Along Main Street are the Custom House, the Nelson House, and the Session House, all dating from the 18th century or earlier. Within a block of Main Street are Grace Episcopal Church, originally built in 1697, and two other colonial buildings. Another group of buildings has been reconstructed by the National Park Service on the original foundations, and an effort is being made to have new construction in the town harmonize with the existing colonial types. Near the east end of Main Street is the Yorktown Victory Monument, erected by the United States to commemorate the French alliance and the victory over Cornwallis. The cornerstone of this monument was laid in 1881 at the celebration of the centennial of the surrender.

Near Yorktown lie the remains of the British earthworks of 1781, modified and strengthened by the Confederate forces during the Civil War. A few hundred yards beyond them are reconstructed parts of the French and American lines. The original allied works were leveled on Washington's orders immediately after the siege, but reconstruction of the more significant parts has been possible through careful investigation and documentary research. In several of the reconstructed batteries are mounted guns of the American Revolution period, including some that were used at the siege of Yorktown. Highways and park roads through the battlefield lead to the encampment and headquarters areas of the French and American armies.

The victory at Yorktown came 174 years after the founding of Jamestown, which is only 23 miles away. Midway between Yorktown and Jamestown is Williamsburg, where colonial life in Virginia reached a peak. There, strong leadership in the quest for independence developed. Together, Jamestown, Williamsburg, and Yorktown help reveal much of the story of our colonial period in Virginia.

*Reading Time*_____ *Comprehension Score*_____ *Words per Minute*_____

Recalling Facts

1. Yorktown was established during the early
   - ☐ a. 1690s.
   - ☐ b. 1720s.
   - ☐ c. 1740s.

2. Yorktown prospered because of its trade in
   - ☐ a. tobacco.
   - ☐ b. glass.
   - ☐ c. pewter.

3. The church mentioned in the article is
   - ☐ a. Baptist.
   - ☐ b. Methodist.
   - ☐ c. Episcopal.

4. The Yorktown Victory Monument commemorates the alliance with
   - ☐ a. Germany.
   - ☐ b. France.
   - ☐ c. Canada.

5. Which one of the following towns is not mentioned?
   - ☐ a. Jamestown
   - ☐ b. Williamsburg
   - ☐ c. Roanoke

Understanding the Passage

6. The National Park Service is the agency that has
   - ☐ a. established campsites near historic Yorktown.
   - ☐ b. cleared land for a new visitor's center in Yorktown.
   - ☐ c. reconstructed buildings in Yorktown.

7. Ideas are presented according to order of
   - ☐ a. time.
   - ☐ b. importance.
   - ☐ c. interest.

8. Yorktown is considered a historic town because
   - ☐ a. two wars have been fought in its vicinity.
   - ☐ b. many famous people have lived in the town.
   - ☐ c. it was the first capital of the United States.

9. The author states that Yorktown
   - ☐ a. had a larger population in colonial days.
   - ☐ b. was the scene of a decisive Civil War battle.
   - ☐ c. was nearly destroyed by a fire.

10. We can conclude that
    - ☐ a. Virginia is a state of historic significance.
    - ☐ b. George Washington was a fearless leader.
    - ☐ c. battles are often fought on sacred soil.

Early Hunters

What the early hunters may have looked like no one really knows, for archaeologists have not found a single undisputed trace of their physical remains. Skeletal fragments of what might be early man in this country have turned up in several places, but usually geologists, archaeologists, and others cannot agree as to just how ancient these remains might be. One candidate for the honor of "earliest man" yet found in America was discovered in 1953 near Midland, Texas. Actually, these remains were those of a female. They were found under geologic conditions that might indicate considerable age and in indirect association with types of arti-facts that are dated as being of Folsom age or slightly more recent. It is not positive, however, that "Midland Man" is the oldest known American. Many anthropologists believe that the earliest people in this country were of Asiatic descent and thus might well have looked like some of the modern American Indians.

We do not even know if they used animal skins as clothing. With a rather cool, damp climate, we can assume that they had some sort of shelter and some types of body covering. It may have been nothing more than generous swabbings of bear grease. Today, near the tip of South America, a tribe of Indians—the Ona—exist in a very damp, cold climate. Eating mostly fish and sea mammals, they live in crude brush shelters and wear little if any clothing most of the time. In Africa, certain primitive Pygmy tribes hunt game as large as giraffes with small bows and arrows. They surround their quarry first and then follow it, often for days, until they can bring down the weary animal at close range with their spears.

Perhaps that is how the early hunters in America survived. We cannot be certain, but scattered around the Four Corners country are a few sites where spear points, scrapers, and other tools have been found under conditions indicating great age. In other cases throughout the greater Southwest, points have been found deep in the remains of slaughtered animals of now extinct species. Often these remains are found in ancient swamps and waterholes, where it had been possible to trap or mire the animals and finally kill them. Fortunately, the mucky swampland has helped preserve the bones so that today the archaeologist can tell the story of how they were killed.

Recalling Facts

1. What early hunters looked
   like is based on
   - □ a. facts.
   - □ b. theory.
   - □ c. proof.

2. One candidate for the
   distinction of America's
   "earliest man" was found in
   - □ a. Kansas.
   - □ b. Michigan.
   - □ c. Texas.

3. The "earliest man" uncovered
   in the early 1950s was a
   - □ a. child.
   - □ b. man.
   - □ c. woman.

4. Many scientists believe that
   the earliest inhabitants of
   America were
   - □ a. European.
   - □ b. Asian.
   - □ c. African.

5. Early hunters often trapped
   their animals in
   - □ a. canyons.
   - □ b. ravines.
   - □ c. swamps.

Understanding the Passage

6. Anthropologists are quite certain
   that some of America's early men
   - □ a. lived in a cool, damp climate.
   - □ b. wore animal skins.
   - □ c. used bows and arrows.

7. The reference to the Ona Indians
   of South America proves that
   - □ a. primitive people are mainly
     vegetarians.
   - □ b. hunting techniques have
     become very sophisticated.
   - □ c. people in cool climates do not
     necessarily wear heavy clothes.

8. The article suggests that much
   conjecture about early hunters
   - □ a. is the result of computer
     analysis.
   - □ b. comes from a study of primi-
     tive tribes in the world today.
   - □ c. is based on animal remains
     unearthed near the Arctic
     Circle.

9. The tone of this selection is
   generally
   - □ a. informative.
   - □ b. humorous.
   - □ c. critical.

10. We may conclude that
    - □ a. the origins of early man will
      never be discovered.
    - □ b. scientists will continue looking
      for evidence of early man.
    - □ c. scientists will concentrate their
      search in the Northwest.

Andersonville, the largest and best known of Southern military prisons, was located in Sumter County, Georgia. It was established after Confederate officials decided that the large number of Union soldiers being held in Richmond prisons should be moved elsewhere because they were a serious drain on the city's dwindling food supply. Also, the Northern captives would become a liability in the event of an enemy attack.

In their search for a suitable prison site, Confederate authorities hoped to find a place more remote from the theater of war, where the prisoners could be more easily guarded, where enemy raids would be less likely, and where food could be more readily obtained. In December 1863, after ruling out several likely locations in Virginia and North Carolina, they finally settled on the Georgia site bacause of "its nearness to the railroad, the presence of a large supply of beautiful, clear water, and the healthful climate."

At that time, the site of Andersonville was a small community of about twenty people. The only buildings were a depot, a church, a store, a cotton warehouse, and about a dozen houses, most of which were shanties.

Confederate soldiers and slaves from neighborhood plantations began clearing the land for the prison in January 1864. For the next six weeks, the hillsides echoed to the ring of axes, the crash of trees, the thud of shovels, and the shouts of men as the sandy Georgia soil was stripped of its lofty pines. The trees were trimmed and topped to make logs about twenty feet long. These were then hewed to a thickness of 8 to 12 inches and set vertically five feet into the ground to form an almost inpregnable stockaded enclosure, encircling 16½ acres of land.

Sentry boxes, or "pigeon-roosts" as the prisoners called them, were positioned at intervals along the top of the stockade. They afforded the guards a comfortable place in which to stand and watch what was going on inside the pen. A deadline was established inside the stockade and parallel to the fence. It was marked by a wood railing over which no prisoner was allowed to go, day or night, under penalty of being shot. The ground between the deadline and the fence was called the deadrun. A stream flowed west to east through the prison yard, dividing it roughly in half.

Recalling Facts

1. Andersonville was located in
   - ☐ a. North Carolina.
   - ☐ b. Mississippi.
   - ☐ c. Georgia.

2. Prisoners who occupied Andersonville had been moved from
   - ☐ a. New York City.
   - ☐ b. Atlanta.
   - ☐ c. Richmond.

3. Andersonville prison was built because of
   - ☐ a. low food supplies.
   - ☐ b. uncontrollable behavior.
   - ☐ c. overcrowded conditions.

4. How long did men work to clear the land and build the stockade?
   - ☐ a. two weeks
   - ☐ b. six weeks
   - ☐ c. ten weeks

5. The prison covered an area larger than
   - ☐ a. 16 acres.
   - ☐ b. 25 acres.
   - ☐ c. 52 acres.

Understanding the Passage

6. "Pigeon-roosts" were actually
   - ☐ a. torture rooms.
   - ☐ b. training areas.
   - ☐ c. lookout posts.

7. Andersonville was named after a
   - ☐ a. small town.
   - ☐ b. famous novel.
   - ☐ c. celebrated general.

8. The designers of Andersonville believed that it was
   - ☐ a. a modern prison with many conveniences.
   - ☐ b. far removed from advancing enemy troops.
   - ☐ c. able to withstand severe storms.

9. The author implies that Andersonville had a good supply of
   - ☐ a. clean water.
   - ☐ b. fresh meat.
   - ☐ c. native fruit.

10. The author is mostly concerned with
   - ☐ a. the intolerable living conditions at Andersonville.
   - ☐ b. the construction of Andersonville.
   - ☐ c. prison camps during the Civil War.

In recent years, the need to preserve the vestiges of humankind's past has resulted in the development of conservation as a science. The work is extremely diverse, but it is divided into one of four fields: the conservation of historical sites, of buildings, of artworks, and of museum artifacts. The conservator strives to retain the material with which she or he is dealing in its original condition and to make necessary additions or changes for preservation purposes.

Historical sites can be affected by shifting environmental conditions. At Mohenjo-Daro, a prehistoric city in India's Indus Valley excavated in the early twentieth century, the rising water table in the valley has led to water seepage into the mud brick construction of the buildings. The evaporation of groundwater on the surface of these structures has caused their disintegration. The suggested conservation procedure is to sink bore holes for pumps throughout the site to lower the water table.

Sites are usually threatened by normal weathering. One type of protection is to raise a temporary roof over the site as was done at a Roman villa in Italy. Reconstruction of the buildings may occur when the foundations exist such as at Colonial Williamsburg. The relocation of a monument to a new site may also occur, as in the case of the rock-cut facade of the Egyptian temple of Abu Simbel that would have been submerged by the waters of the Aswan Dam.

The conservation of buildings is usually undertaken by architects and conservators who must undergo training to learn historic construction methods. Some buildings in need of conservation suffer only from neglect and can be easily restored, while others have been damaged by alterations and additions. Through research on comparable buildings and original architectural designs and by means of contemporary pictures or descriptions, these may be restored to their original condition.

Environmental conditions may also cause the rapid decay of buildings. The marble exterior of the Acropolis in Athens, Greece, is deteriorating because of the sulphur dioxide in the atmospheric pollution. No satisfactory solution has been found, although the marble may be chemically treated to render it less soluble.

Subsidence is also a serious conservation problem. In Venice, where a gradual geological structural change has resulted in the sinking of the islands on which this city is built, the problem is one of great magnitude. A possible answer may lie in the building of cofferdams around the city and continuous pumping to lower the water.

Recalling Facts

1. Historical sites may be adversely affected by
   - ☐ a. visitors.
   - ☐ b. conservation methods.
   - ☐ c. the environment.

2. A temporary roof was raised over a site in
   - ☐ a. Italy.
   - ☐ b. Williamsburg.
   - ☐ c. Egypt.

3. Mohenjo-Daro is located in
   - ☐ a. Africa.
   - ☐ b. India.
   - ☐ c. southern Europe.

4. The temple of Abu Simbel was "rescued" by
   - ☐ a. temporary storage.
   - ☐ b. relocation.
   - ☐ c. chemical treatment.

5. Subsidence is another term meaning to
   - ☐ a. sink.
   - ☐ b. provide food.
   - ☐ c. erode.

Understanding the Passage

6. When possible, a goal of conservation is to
   - ☐ a. retain the object in its original condition.
   - ☐ b. make the object look new.
   - ☐ c. always repair the object.

7. The facade of the Acropolis has mainly deteriorated because of
   - ☐ a. too many visitors to the site.
   - ☐ b. the high levels of atmospheric pollutants.
   - ☐ c. the theft of many parts of the structure.

8. Venice has been sinking over the centuries because of
   - ☐ a. the growing population.
   - ☐ b. the water pollution.
   - ☐ c. a geological structural change.

9. Colonial Williamsburg is an example of historical site
   - ☐ a. reconstruction.
   - ☐ b. relocation.
   - ☐ c. alteration.

10. Conservation is considered to be
    - ☐ a. a science.
    - ☐ b. an art.
    - ☐ c. a technology.

50 Poison Ivy

Poison ivy is a name commonly used to describe several kinds of harmful vines and shrubs that are related to sumac. These vines and shrubs can be found almost anywhere in the United States or southern Canada. Although they may appear in various forms, all of the plants contain a poisonous oil similar to carbolic acid that is extremely irritating to the human skin. Because these plants are nearly everywhere, anyone who ventures into a wooded area or an open field should learn to recognize poison ivy.

Depending on what region of the country you are living in, poison ivy might appear differently than it does in other places. The vine variety is the most common manifestation of the plant, and it is frequently seen growing on other host plants. Another variety that is particularly prevalent in the southern states and on the Pacific coast appears as a bush rather than a vine. But despite differences in growing patterns, both bushy and climbing types of poison ivy have identical leaves. Although seasonal changes affect their coloration, the distinctive leaves are always made up of three smaller leaflets creating a roughly triangular shape. These leaves appear unusually shiny when compared to any other plants surrounding them.

Despite regular efforts that have been made to destroy poison ivy, usually by uprooting it or spraying it with herbicides, the plant is still so comon that these methods have clearly been ineffective in controlling its growth. Therefore, most people will probably come into contact with it at one time or another. Unless you are especially sensitive to it, certain measures can ensure minimal irritation from poison ivy oil. As soon as you realize that you have touched poison ivy, wash the affected area thoroughly, for the oil's penetration generally takes a certain amount of time. Do not allow any part of that affected area to touch another section of skin. If you are unable to prevent contamination, you will soon notice itching blisters beginning to develop. They may be treated externally with calamine lotion, Epsom salts, or bicarbonate of soda. In severe cases, doctors may prescribe more powerful dermatological ointments. Although a poison ivy vaccine has been developed, it is only effective if taken before exposure. The best method of prevention is an observant eye. If you can recognize poison ivy, you will be better able to stay away from it.

Recalling Facts

1. Poison ivy is related to which plant?
   - ☐ a. nightshade
   - ☐ b. hemlock
   - ☐ c. sumac

2. Carbolic acid is
   - ☐ a. only found in climbing plants.
   - ☐ b. used in making calamine lotion.
   - ☐ c. irritating to the human skin.

3. Poison ivy leaves form
   - ☐ a. circular clusters.
   - ☐ b. rough triangles.
   - ☐ c. irregular patterns.

4. The best way to remove poison ivy oil from skin is with
   - ☐ a. surgical procedures.
   - ☐ b. Epsom salts.
   - ☐ c. soap and water.

5. Poison ivy vaccines are effective if taken
   - ☐ a. before exposure.
   - ☐ b. during exposure.
   - ☐ c. after exposure.

Understanding the Passage

6. Poison ivy plants
   - ☐ a. always appear identical.
   - ☐ b. can grow in different ways.
   - ☐ c. have never been seen in Canada.

7. Poison ivy is resistant to
   - ☐ a. bulldozers.
   - ☐ b. water.
   - ☐ c. herbicides.

8. Some people
   - ☐ a. cultivate poison ivy.
   - ☐ b. are especially sensitive to poison ivy oil.
   - ☐ c. believe that poison ivy has medicinal uses.

9. Bicarbonate of soda can be used to
   - ☐ a. treat itching blisters.
   - ☐ b. kill poison ivy plants.
   - ☐ c. produce a climbing variety of sumac.

10. You can best avoid poison ivy by
   - ☐ a. moving to the Pacific coast.
   - ☐ b. walking in open fields.
   - ☐ c. knowing how to identify the plant.

Answer Key

Progress Graph

Pacing Graph

Answer Key

1	1. b	2. c	3. c	4. b	5. b	6. a	7. b	8. c	9. a	10. b
2	1. b	2. a	3. b	4. c	5. a	6. c	7. a	8. b	9. b	10. a
3	1. b	2. c	3. a	4. c	5. c	6. b	7. a	8. b	9. a	10. c
4	1. b	2. c	3. b	4. a	5. b	6. a	7. b	8. c	9. a	10. a
5	1. a	2. b	3. b	4. c	5. b	6. a	7. c	8. b	9. b	10. c
6	1. b	2. c	3. c	4. a	5. a	6. a	7. c	8. b	9. b	10. a
7	1. a	2. b	3. a	4. c	5. a	6. a	7. b	8. a	9. b	10. b
8	1. c	2. c	3. a	4. c	5. b	6. b	7. b	8. a	9. b	10. c
9	1. b	2. c	3. a	4. b	5. a	6. c	7. c	8. c	9. a	10. b
10	1. c	2. b	3. c	4. a	5. a	6. c	7. b	8. a	9. b	10. a
11	1. a	2. b	3. c	4. b	5. a	6. b	7. c	8. a	9. b	10. a
12	1. b	2. b	3. a	4. c	5. b	6. c	7. a	8. b	9. a	10. b
13	1. a	2. c	3. c	4. c	5. b	6. a	7. b	8. b	9. a	10. a
14	1. b	2. a	3. a	4. b	5. c	6. c	7. b	8. c	9. c	10. a
15	1. c	2. b	3. b	4. c	5. a	6. a	7. b	8. c	9. c	10. c
16	1. c	2. b	3. a	4. b	5. c	6. b	7. b	8. a	9. c	10. c
17	1. c	2. c	3. c	4. a	5. c	6. b	7. a	8. a	9. b	10. c
18	1. a	2. c	3. b	4. c	5. b	6. b	7. b	8. a	9. c	10. b
19	1. a	2. b	3. a	4. b	5. a	6. b	7. b	8. b	9. c	10. c
20	1. a	2. b	3. b	4. b	5. b	6. a	7. b	8. a	9. c	10. c
21	1. c	2. b	3. a	4. c	5. b	6. a	7. a	8. b	9. a	10. a
22	1. c	2. c	3. a	4. a	5. c	6. a	7. a	8. a	9. b	10. b
23	1. a	2. c	3. c	4. b	5. a	6. b	7. a	8. c	9. a	10. c
24	1. a	2. b	3. a	4. b	5. c	6. a	7. a	8. b	9. a	10. c
25	1. c	2. b	3. b	4. c	5. a	6. a	7. c	8. b	9. a	10. b

26	1. b	2. a	3. b	4. c	5. a	6. b	7. a	8. b	9. c	10. a
27	1. b	2. a	3. a	4. c	5. c	6. c	7. a	8. b	9. a	10. b
28	1. b	2. b	3. c	4. c	5. a	6. b	7. a	8. c	9. a	10. b
29	1. b	2. b	3. b	4. a	5. a	6. b	7. c	8. a	9. a	10. b
30	1. c	2. a	3. b	4. b	5. b	6. b	7. c	8. b	9. b	10. c
31	1. c	2. a	3. b	4. a	5. b	6. c	7. c	8. a	9. c	10. c
32	1. c	2. a	3. c	4. b	5. a	6. a	7. b	8. b	9. c	10. a
33	1. c	2. a	3. c	4. b	5. b	6. b	7. a	8. c	9. b	10. a
34	1. a	2. b	3. b	4. c	5. c	6. b	7. b	8. a	9. b	10. a
35	1. b	2. b	3. a	4. c	5. a	6. c	7. a	8. c	9. b	10. b
36	1. c	2. a	3. c	4. b	5. a	6. b	7. c	8. a	9. c	10. a
37	1. b	2. a	3. a	4. c	5. b	6. c	7. b	8. a	9. a	10. b
38	1. a	2. b	3. a	4. a	5. a	6. c	7. a	8. a	9. c	10. a
39	1. b	2. b	3. c	4. a	5. b	6. c	7. a	8. a	9. b	10. c
40	1. a	2. b	3. a	4. c	5. b	6. b	7. c	8. a	9. b	10. c
41	1. a	2. b	3. c	4. b	5. c	6. b	7. c	8. b	9. b	10. a
42	1. c	2. c	3. b	4. b	5. b	6. c	7. a	8. b	9. c	10. b
43	1. c	2. a	3. b	4. c	5. b	6. a	7. b	8. b	9. a	10. c
44	1. b	2. c	3. a	4. c	5. b	6. c	7. a	8. b	9. b	10. c
45	1. b	2. a	3. a	4. a	5. b	6. a	7. b	8. b	9. c	10. a
46	1. a	2. a	3. c	4. b	5. c	6. c	7. a	8. a	9. a	10. a
47	1. b	2. c	3. c	4. b	5. c	6. a	7. c	8. b	9. a	10. b
48	1. c	2. c	3. a	4. b	5. a	6. c	7. a	8. b	9. a	10. b
49	1. c	2. a	3. b	4. b	5. a	6. a	7. b	8. c	9. a	10. a
50	1. c	2. c	3. b	4. c	5. a	6. b	7. c	8. b	9. a	10. c

Progress Graph (1–25)

Directions: Write your comprehension score in the box under the selection number. Then put an x on the line above each box to show your reading time and words-per-minute reading rate.

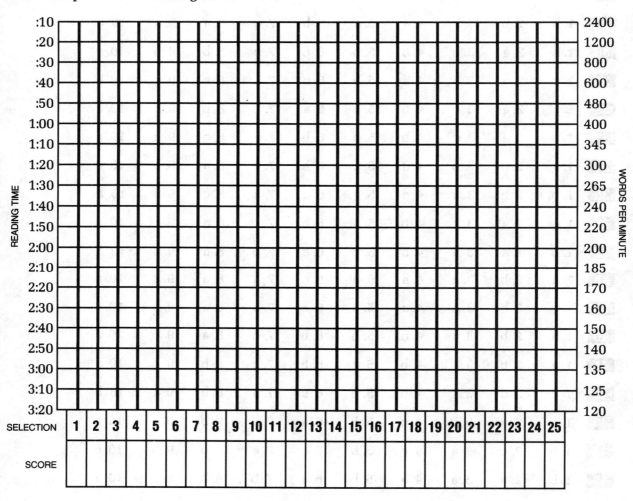

READING TIME		WORDS PER MINUTE
:10		2400
:20		1200
:30		800
:40		600
:50		480
1:00		400
1:10		345
1:20		300
1:30		265
1:40		240
1:50		220
2:00		200
2:10		185
2:20		170
2:30		160
2:40		150
2:50		140
3:00		135
3:10		125
3:20		120

SELECTION	1	2	3	4	5	6	7	8	9	10	11	12	13	14	15	16	17	18	19	20	21	22	23	24	25
SCORE																									

Progress Graph (26–50)

Directions: Write your comprehension score in the box under the selection number. Then put an x on the line above each box to show your reading time and words-per-minute reading rate.

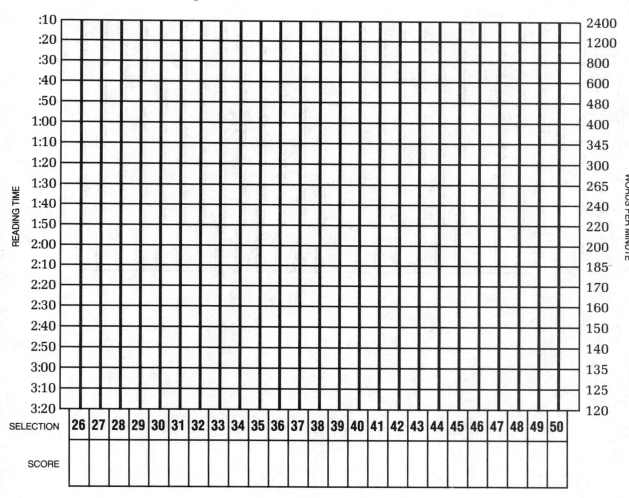

READING TIME		WORDS PER MINUTE
:10		2400
:20		1200
:30		800
:40		600
:50		480
1:00		400
1:10		345
1:20		300
1:30		265
1:40		240
1:50		220
2:00		200
2:10		185
2:20		170
2:30		160
2:40		150
2:50		140
3:00		135
3:10		125
3:20		120

SELECTION: 26 27 28 29 30 31 32 33 34 35 36 37 38 39 40 41 42 43 44 45 46 47 48 49 50

SCORE

Pacing Graph

Directions: In the boxes labeled "Pace" along the bottom of the graph, write your words-per-minute rate. On the vertical line above each box, put an x to indicate your comprehension score.

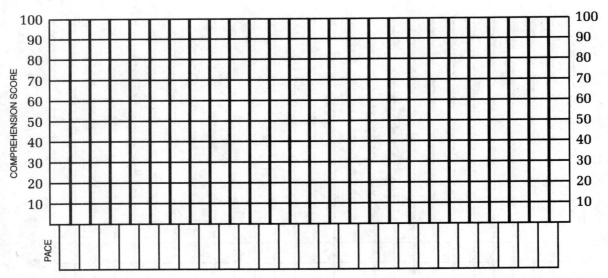